DE PROPRIETATIBUS LITTERARUM

edenda curat

C. H. VAN SCHOONEVELD

Indiana University

Series Practica, 26

A CERTAIN ORDER

The Development of
Herbert Read's Theory of Poetry

by

WORTH TRAVIS HARDER

State University of New York
College of Arts and Science at Geneseo

1971

MOUTON

THE HAGUE · PARIS

To Edith

PREFACE

Sir Herbert Read's achievements were so diverse and his writings so many, that to approach his work from a single direction is necessarily to exclude a great deal. I trace here a line which appears to me fundamental, and with reluctance pass by much else of interest.

The study was in its original form a doctoral dissertation at the University of Michigan, and I have Professor Norman E. Nelson to thank for many kindnesses and much patience and understanding.

I have been assisted by a Faculty Research Fellowship from the Joint Awards Council, University Awards Committee of the State University of New York.

W. T. H.

Geneseo, New York

TABLE OF CONTENTS

INTRODUCTION

The object of this study is to trace a pattern of development in the
critical writings of Sir Herbert Read, particularly during the
formative years 1918—1938. Beginning when anti-romantic ideas
and attitudes that accompanied the rise of modern poetry prevailed,
Read – almost alone among critics of those two decades – made
his way to an avowedly romantic position. He attempted to shape
a poetic theory by means of which he could ground modern poetry
in the central tradition of English romanticism. I propose to show
here the logic of his development.

To speak of 'logic' in relation to the erratic and often contradictory
course Read pursued may seem strange; certainly he was as well
known for his inconsistencies as his consistencies. Perhaps the
usual view of him is that he was in the 1920's a follower of Eliot,
an apostle of 'reason' and 'form' and that in the 1930's he declared
himself a romantic and proceeded to embrace surrealism and
anarchism. This view is not altogether wrong, but it ignores the
thread of consistency which makes his work all of a piece. Read
himself never greatly helped us to see his development as a whole.
He had a habit of shrugging off his inconsistencies as the consequence
of his 'cult of sincerity'. The pattern he saw in his own growth
was something deeper than intellectual: his consistency, he believed,
was a consistency of 'personality', and his inconsistencies arose
from his honesty and sincerity. When he collected his critical
pieces in a book, he was not embarrassed by the variety of viewpoints that might thus be assembled. In *The Tenth Muse*, for
example, he explained that he did not "claim the virtue of consistency". "I am sure a logician could have fine intellectual sport in
exposing my contradictions – my paralogisms, as he might call
them ..... I am a pluralist, content to let loose a number of
truths with no desire to bring them into a house of correction, no

itch to reduce them to some 'unifying formula'."[1] His general outlook, he said, might be stated in this way:

Never yield to habit, especially to habits of thought which polish away
the rough edges of truth; remain open, innocent, original. Put away
childish things, but retain, all the same, a core of childhood, a slender
vein of vital sap which the rings of growth may hide, but must never
destroy. Keep a reserve of simplicity, even of primitiveness, so that
you do not meet elementary situations with sophistication. Your aim
should be, not simply to be, but rather to be ever capable of becoming
– not at rest, but moving with the moving world – always in touch
with what is changing, changing oneself – open, like the child, to the
whole world without but with an inward reserve which the child does
not yet possess, where one gathers a little strength, a certain order.[2]

Certainly much of Read's charm lay in just this candor, this honesty,
this cultivated naïveté underlying an immense sophistication.
In the midst of the often over-rigorous analyses of contemporary
literary criticism, Read came, believing that the essential critical
act is sympathy – to SUBMIT oneself to the work of art. He said,
"The critic with a head but without love, is the monster who
killed Keats. He has had a numerous progeny, and I fancy that
the species has found a particularly congenial habitat in American
universities (but we have enough to spare for export in England)."[3]
Yet there is a pattern to Read's development which is more
than simply the pattern of his personality. While I have no 'unifying formula' capable of reducing everything to order, I have found
through his work a remarkable consistency in his view of poetry as
a primary kind of apprehension and of the poetic process as a
single, instantaneous, non-deliberative act. This conception of
poetry and the poetic process remained constant, no matter how
much his other ideas shifted around. Indeed, the great variety
of ideas Read assembled – philosophical, scientific, sociological,
psychological – fall into place around his view of poetry and the poetic process. All, that is, were selected to buttress his notion of poetry
as a mode of apprehension, absolutely different in its process and
its form from the rational mode. Poetry was for Read a STATE
OF MIND, and any idea that appeared to support this view was

[1] "On Something in Particular", *The Tenth Muse* (London, 1957), p. 4.
[2] *Ibid.*
[3] "The Faith of a Critic", *The Tenth Muse*, p. 325. Originally published
as "The Critic as Man of Feeling", *Kenyon Review*, XII, 4 (1950), 575—580.

liable to be used by him. In turn, almost everything in Read's work can be referred back to his absolute distinction between the poetic and the rational modes of cognition.

The poetic process was for Read essentially a single, visionary act, and all conscious technique, all deliberate construction, was not properly a part of that creative act. It was this assumption that set him apart from the dominant line in Anglo-American criticism, extending from T. S. Eliot through I. A. Richards to the new critics (a line to which Read in some other ways belonged). For in the contextualist approach of the new critics, technique is the means for bringing the poetic essence into being. To Read, however, technique was always in some way elaborative of a poetic essence already there. The forming process occurs somewhere below the level at which conscious construction takes place. Read's approach combined a very severe formalism with a very romantic expressionism: his preoccupation with form, that is, led him not to an analysis of technique but to a study of the forming process deep in the poetic self whence comes the poet's unique knowledge of reality. Now it is difficult to bring formalism and expressionism together. To value the poem as an expression of the poet's mind or personality, or of the soul of the race or nation, or of the mythic mind of humanity, is one thing; to value it as form, existing objectively, is another. Much of Read's theoretical work can be seen as an attempt to hold these two viewpoints together. I trace here the way in which he worked out his poetics, in the conviction that once this is done his significance for contemporary criticism may become more apparent than it has been. I see his peculiar value as a demonstration of what the consequences of a doctrine of poetry as knowledge can be when thoroughly and boldly carried out.

Read's literary criticism falls for the most part into the two divisions under which he grouped his collected essays: "General Theories", and "Particular Studies". My concern here is primarily with the general theories. His particular studies of writers and their works contain perceptive and valuable insights; some of them are minor classics of criticism. But he was never content with this kind of critical activity. From the beginning he insisted on constructing a poetics to which everything could be referred. He was fundamentally a philosophical critic, and it is by his theory that he finally attains significance. Yet to trace the theory through his writings is not easy, in view of his openness and receptivity to ideas and influences, his willingness to contradict himself with equanimity, his intention of remaining always "capable of becoming". My method has been to examine closely, and in chronological order, those of his critical writings which show the development of the theory. This has never been done. A beginning was made by H. W. Häusermann,[4] but his essay, although helpful, was written in the 1930's and does not attempt to consider the theory in detail. A more recent study by Solomon Fishman[5] considers Read's poetics and its place in contemporary criticism but does not do much with its development. I maintain that to see the theory clearly and to assess its significance one has to track Read closely, especially through the years between the two world wars. To quote him out of context is even more hazardous than it is with most critics. For one must take into account not only the context of a particular essay but the current state of Read's ideas. And one cannot rely to any great extent on his own remarks about his development – a situation not surprising in view of his frequent (and sometimes silent) revision of his work. The best plan is to go directly to the works themselves and see what pattern can be made of them. This I have attempted to do.

The reader should expect, then, an attempt to follow Read in his process of "becoming", of "moving with the moving world". To follow him thus, I believe, is to discover a neglected but important chapter in the history of modern Anglo-American literary criticism, and to see the doctrine of poetry as knowledge from an unusual and revealing perspective. Part One deals with the years from 1918, when Read's first essay in poetic theory appeared, to 1932, when *Form in Modern Poetry* was published. Part Two covers his subsequent development, particularly during the 1930's. By the end of the 1930's he had worked out most of the implications for poetry of his neo-romantic position, and thereafter turned

---

[4] H. W. Häusermann, "The Development of Herbert Read", in *Herbert Read: An Introduction to his Work by Various Hands*, ed. Henry Treece (London, 1944).

[5] Solomon Fishman, "Sir Herbert Read: Poetics vs. Criticism", *Journal of Aesthetics and Art Criticism*, XIII, 2 (1954). There are few good studies of Read's poetics. Fishman's and Häusermann's are the best. Francis Berry's monograph, *Herbert Read* (London, 1945), gives an overall view of his work but is not particularly critical.

increasingly to the plastic arts, general aesthetics, and social and educational philosophy. Only in *The True Voice of Feeling* (1953) did he make a major elaboration of his poetic theory. My argument is somewhat winding, but necessarily so because of the nature of the subject. It should be borne in mind, too, that the subject is the development of Read's theory of poetry, not his theory of art or politics or education, or his philosophy of life, although I am naturally led to some extent into all those areas. With Read, all theory begins in poetry. Finally, while it may appear at times that I treat Read as if I were "the monster who killed Keats", my interest in him actually springs from the heart, not the head. I do not always agree with him, but I begin with sympathy and end, I hope, in understanding.

PART ONE

VISION AND FORM

I

POETRY AS VISION

1

For the beginnings of Herbert Read's poetic theory one must go to the essays and reviews which he contributed between 1917 and 1920 to the journal, *Art and Letters*.[1] His theory, like his poetic practice, grew out of the Imagist movement, and the influence of Imagist doctrine is everywhere apparent in these early writings. Of all the poet-critics associated with the rise of modern poetry, Read was the most faithful to Imagist ideals. Yet there was from the beginning an emphasis in Read's theory different from that of the Imagists, and in this difference lay the seed of his subsequent development.

The Imagist movement appeared first of all as a revolution in technique: forms and conventions of the immediate past were discarded in an attempt to achieve a more precise and accurate means of expression. Most of the critical writings connected with the movement were concerned with the defense of the Imagists' technical innovations, particularly their metrical principles of 'cadence' and 'free verse', since it was on this point that they had encountered the greatest misunderstanding from the public and the most resistance from academic critics. What these new poets had to express, however, was not nearly so clear as was the means of expression they had chosen. The most recent historian of the movement, Stanley Coffman, notes that "when Pound published the principles of Imagism in 1913 . . . he did not mention subject matter; the principles were all technical, having to do with the form of expression rather than with content. And the same may be said generally of the manifestoes published in the anthologies

---

[1] This journal, a quarterly review, was founded by Read and Frank Rutter. Read, while still in the army in France, served as joint editor. See *Annals of Innocence and Experience* (London, 1946), pp. 191—192.

of 1915 and 1916''.[2] Coffman sees the movement as part of a general aesthetic tendency toward the formal, the anti-vital, the non-representational, and he thinks the Imagist poets may have suffered from their lack of a 'message'. "Perhaps", he says, "the interest in the nonrepresentational was an admission that the artist really had little of significance to say: perhaps the 'dehumanization' of art was, as some insist, a token of defeat. But the new concerns at least provided some excuse for a re-examination of the fundamentals of expression, and this, in turn, gave them some excuse, which they could not find in their 'message', for continuing to write and paint, for continuing to exist as artists . . . .".[3]

However true this may have been for the Imagists – and the many calls to arms of the movement would seem to indicate that the poets themselves did not always see the 'dehumanization' of art as a 'token of defeat' – it was certainly not true for Read. The one point that stands out in his frequently confused and contradictory writings for *Art and Letters* is his preoccupation with the SIGNIFICANCE of the new poetry. The poet's 'vision', not his technique, was for Read the supreme consideration and he complained that the Imagists had too often failed to achieve significance because of the inadequacy of their vision. Exactly what Read meant by 'vision' – and by a number of other terms he used – is never very clear, except that it had to do with a peculiarly aesthetic knowledge of reality. But this is just the point. For in his conviction that the poet was either a revealer of knowledge or nothing, Read was going to the heart of the problem of the significance of the new poetry. There lay, in fact, behind the Imagists' "re-examination of the fundamentals of expression" a major reorientation in poetry. The image had come to assume in itself a cognitive significance. Against the discursive, analytical knowledge provided by 'science', the image stood as the expression of a nondiscursive, synthetic apprehension of reality. The innovations of the new poetry rested on an assumption that the poet, through a unique use of language, can present a fresh and pure vision of the world, stripping away the abstractions of conceptual thought and revealing reality in its nakedness.

[2] Stanley K. Coffman, *Imagism, A Chapter for the History of Modern Poetry* (Norman, 1951), p. 213.
[3] *Ibid.*, pp. 213–214.

This theoretical or philosophical rationale for the new poetry has been the subject of much recent study,[4] and it may be that we understand it today more clearly than some of the poets did. Certainly Coffman is right in pointing out that the new poets were for the most part less interested in establishing theoretically the significance of what they were doing than in solving the problems of expression immediately before them. The only real theorist of the Imagist movement was T. E. Hulme, who in the years just before the war had begun to construct a theory of the image, using an aesthetic derived from Bergson and a rationale for abstract form taken from Worringer, the German art historian. But Hulme died in the war, and his work, although influential on Pound, was not widely known until his posthumous papers were published in 1924 (under Read's editorship). How much of Hulme's work Read had seen in 1918, when he wrote his first theoretical essay, "Definitions towards a Modern Theory of Poetry", I do not know. At any rate, there is none of Hulme's preoccupation with LANGUAGE in Read's essay. Instead there is a kind of mystical aestheticism which seems almost more appropriate to a visual medium than to poetry. Sometimes the reader is hard put to understand just what Read had in mind. One thing, nevertheless, is clear: Read was attempting not merely to discuss the form of expression, as the Imagists had mostly done, but to establish the significance of that form. His point throughout was that the form of expression only attains significance when the poet's vision is significant, and it was to a mysterious relationship in the poetic process between form and vision that he chiefly addressed himself. He seemed to be saying that form was a product of vision: that the forming process and the visionary process were essentially the same, while technique was only a subsidiary matter of 'decoration'.

The ideas in this essay and in Read's other contributions to *Art and Letters* seem not only sometimes confused but generally thin and derivative. There are echoes of French symbolist thought, of the Imagist manifestoes, of some of Pound's early pronouncements, and of Clive Bell's theory of 'significant form' in the visual arts. Yet Read had already begun to put his own stamp on these

---

[4] See, *e.g.*, Frank Kermode, *Romantic Image* (London, 1957); Donald Davie, *Articulate Energy* (London, 1955); Graham Hough, *Image and Experience* (London, 1961); C. K. Stead, *The New Poetic* (London, 1964).

ideas, and for this reason his early writings warrant a certain amount of close study. This is particularly true of the "Definitions towards a Modern Theory of Poetry".

This essay opened with three 'axioms' and continued with a series of definitions of terms intended to explain the axioms. It concluded with a short critique of contemporary poetry based on the definitions. The axioms, which Read said "are suggested as dogmas", follow:

1. Form is determined by the emotion which requires expression.
   Corollary: Form is not an unchanging mould into which any emotion can be poured.
2. The poem is an artistic whole demanding strict unity.
3. The criterion of the poem is the quality of the vision expressed, granted that the expression is adequate.
   Corollary: Rhyme, metre, cadence, alliteration, are various decorative devices to be used as the vision demands, and are not formal quantities pre-ordained.[5]

The definitions began with the terms 'emotion' and 'vision':

Emotion or *ecstasy* is the response of the mind to form and colour of environment. Beauty is experienced by the senses – is the fulfilment of an aesthetic lust for colour and fragrance; which fulfilment *may* be a vision to be moulded by the intellect into formal beauty.

By *vision* we mean the recognition of emotions possessing an aesthetic value. We would emphasize "recognition"; this word is not used in its strictly psychological connotation. An emotion is "cognized" by any individual in the sense that it is experienced. A further process, that of the artist, is to relate this "cognition" to the aesthetic absolute, *i.e.* to "recognize" the emotion.

Vision, resulting from emotion, is obviously not an intellectual quantity. Nor, more obviously still, is it an ethical quantity. The only way in which intellect does enter into the visionary process is in a selective way, *e.g.* rejecting emotions that are of no aesthetic value, or the expression of which would be too imitative. Of course, we have long passed the day in which it is necessary to repudiate the doctrine that aesthetic creation demands an ethical sanction. Yet the artist who lacks a high philosophic basis is doomed to damnation, largely because he is precluded from that intellectual selection just mentioned which is so necessary to artistic perfection.[6]

The poetic process, in other words, begins with an emotional response to the 'form and colour of environment'. This emotion

[5] "Definitions towards a Modern Theory of Poetry", *Art and Letters*, I, 3 (1918), 73.
[6] *Ibid.*, 74.

is then 'recognized' through the poet's vision, an act which relates
the original 'cognition' of the emotion to the 'aesthetic absolute'.
The 'recognition' of an emotion seems to result in an AESTHETIZING
of it, transforming it to an aesthetic emotion. There occurs in
connection with this a selection and rejection of emotions according to their aesthetic worth, and evidently the higher the 'philosophic basis' of the poet the more successful this picking and
choosing will be. It is this discrimination, based on past experience
and philosophic knowledge, which Read called 'intellectual',
and this is, according to him, the only way intellect enters the
visionary process. The act of vision is not itself intellectual, nor
is it ethical.

The terms 'unity', 'form', and 'decoration', and finally the poem
itself, Read defined as follows:

By *unity* we mean something akin to the classical dramatic unity'
but modified to suit the vision instead of the drama. So, in place of the
unities of time, place and action, we demand the unity of vision or
idea . . .
Form is the completed architecture of the poem, possessing exact
significance. It should always bear a conjunctive relation to the emotional quality of the vision, and cannot be predetermined without a
sacrifice of unity or vitality . . .
Decoration. Much of the present confusion among poets and critics
arises from an incapacity to distinguish decoration from the essential
vision, even from an ability to see in decoration the essential element
of the poem . . . Decorations in poetry are rhyme, rhythm, metre, cadence,
assonance and alliteration. Nothing so distinguishes and selects the poet
as the appropriate use of decoration. The great majority of English and
French poets use decorative devices without any sense of economy.
For perfect command of decoration in the past we must seek among
the poets of Greece and China and Japan. In our own day we may
find it among the Imagists . . .
The overuse of decoration spoils the poem by sacrificing vitality,
exactness and concentration – essential qualities of perfect expression.
All these qualities are inter-related and are necessary to prevent an
indefinite, indecisive effect – such an effect not being so powerful in
appeal to the aesthetic senses.

Reading these definitions into our axioms, we can now logically define
the poem as follows:

The poem is the expression in words of the mind's vision, and expression, to be effective, must possess significant form, which significant
form is achieved by unity, vitality, exactness, concentration and decoration.[7]

[7] *Ibid.*, 75—77.

Expression, then, follows vision; but where the one ends and the other begins is not very clear in these definitions, nor is the manner in which expression proceeds. The poet expresses his vision, Read said, in a 'significant form', which is achieved by unity, vitality, exactness, concentration, and decoration. Unity the poet achieves by maintaining the unity of the vision; and vitality, exactness, and concentration chiefly by avoiding the overuse of decoration. Intellect, which plays only a selective role in the visionary act, seems to have little to do in expression, unless maintaining the unity of the vision is an intellectual act. Under the term 'decoration' are subsumed most of the technical devices of poetry – rhyme, rhythm, metre, cadence, assonance, alliteration, *etc.* These are to be used "as the vision demands", and Read's comments showed that, with the possible exception of rhythm and cadence, he was not much interested in them:

Rhythm and cadence are closely allied in nature. Rhythm is the modulated flow of stress within the phrase. The appropriate linking of rhythms within the poem makes the cadence of the poem.

Rhyme and metre are arbitrary decorations, and really belong to an age when the poem was indistinguishable from the ballad and written, to be accompanied by music. In rhyme there also enters the rather childishly barbaric love of repetition and jingle – a musical rather than a poetic quantity.

Assonance and alliteration are obvious external decorations not needing any comment.[8]

Yet if these devices are to be used as decorations, what are they to decorate? How, in other words, is the vision itself expressed? Read's definitions do not tell us. For all we can make out, he might as well be writing about visual art. Certainly 'form', as conceived in this essay, seems more spatial than temporal. The traditional conventions associated with poetry as a temporal art, such as regular metrical and sound patterns, have been entirely overthrown, and even rhythm itself relegated to the function of 'decoration'. Read believed, he said, that "the theory of each art is, in the abstract the same; only the material to be worked in differs".[9] We get no adequate conception, however, of how the poet's material differs from the painter's; Read's notion of the poetic 'vision' is so

[8] *Ibid.,* 77.
[9] *Ibid.,* 76.

completely VISUAL that he cannot, or does not think it necessary
to, tell us what the poet 'decorates' with the devices of poetic
art. He uses the term 'significant form' to refer to something in
poetry that seems to be the equivalent of what Clive Bell meant
by the term in the visual arts – certain combinations and arrange-
ments of line and color which arouse in us peculiarly aesthetic
emotions.[10] In poetry this could only be an 'image', in the sense
n which Pound had defined that term: "that which presents an
intellectual and emotional complex in an instant of time".[11] The
one poetic device most relevant to such an end is metaphor, because
it FUSES the terms of a comparison, and it is significant that Read
omitted metaphor from his list of decorations. Evidently he did
not think of metaphor as a 'device'. The 'instantaneous complex',
however, meant more to Read than it did to Pound. For Read, unlike
Pound, seemed uninterested in the temporal art – the 'music' –
of poetry. He distinguished, for example, in his remarks on 'decorations', between a 'musical' and a 'poetic' quantity, the latter
being evidently the nontemporal 'complex' – the image. Actually,
the image was for Read – and this became clearer as his theory
developed – not a matter of 'art' at all. Even in this essay of 1918
we can see that the image is not itself the product of any technical
means, although it may be 'decorated' by technical means. It
belongs to the vision. The image is already there before technique
begins, and the rest of the poetic process is elaboration – 'decoration'. As Read stated in his third axiom, his criterion is the 'quality
of the vision', while expression need only be 'adequate'. It need not
even be communicative; the poet's own satisfaction can be final:

This question only remains doubtful: Does significant expression end
with the artist's satisfaction, or should it necessarily recreate the artist's
vision in another mind? At any rate a relative question, for there is
no equality of aesthetic perception, and the artist can always claim
an aristocracy. And as the artist is essentially (psychologically) an
egoist, his satisfaction is, in one sense, final.[12]

To the general notion of the poetic process outlined in these
definitions Read has clung tenaciously. He has continued to

[10] Clive Bell, *Art* (New York, 1958), p. 17. First published in 1914.

[11] "A Few Don'ts", *Literary Essays of Ezra Pound*, ed. T. S. Eliot (London,
1944), p. 4.

[12] "Definitions . . .", *loc. cit.*, 77.

maintain, in one way or another, that the poetic process does not proceed in time but is confined to an instantaneous seizing or grasping of images; that technique is not a means of discovery but a way of elaborating something which is already there; that form must in no sense be predetermined. And he has continued to have dfficulty in explaining how, finally, form is determined. He had set out in his essay to define the 'essential form' of a poem, but beyond saying that form possesses 'exact significance', bears a 'conjunctive relation' to the emotional quality of the vision, and cannot be predetermined, he leaves us with a very hazy idea of how it is achieved. He speaks of it as a 'completed architecture', and says that the vision is "moulded by the intellect into formal beauty"; this suggests a conscious and deliberate forming and shaping, but in his description of the poetic process any such activity seems to come under the head of mere 'decoration'. How vision becomes form remains a mystery.

Read concluded his essay by applying his definition of the poem to contemporary English poetry. Most of it he found wanting. Only the Imagists, he said, "approach any clarity of creative intention", and even they, "in one or two ways . . . have gone astray".

In their manifestoes they had renounced the decorative word, but their sea-violets and wild hyacinths tend to become as decorative as the beryls and jades of Oscar Wilde. And this criticism of very great importance can be made: They betray a pitiful lack of that aesthetic selection which is the artist's most peculiar duty. In his notes on the modern novel, Henry James has distinguished the "slice" of naturalism of the Arnold Bennett type, and damned it as inartistic. So these Imagists may be accused of expressing a "slice" of their emotions, and of not discriminating between the vision of purely aesthetic value and the vision of emotional value only.[13]

The Imagists were in fact vulnerable to this charge. They had isolated the image by pruning away the discourse in which images had traditionally functioned in poetry. They had presented the image without comment and had often been extraordinarily success-ful in capturing and evoking a particular emotion by this method, but their poems rarely attained any very large significance. T. E. Hulme, indeed, had claimed poetic subjects could be trivial; he had called upon the new poets to turn their backs on generalities and

[13] *Ibid.*, 78.

abstractions, to quit "dragging in the infinite" in the manner of the romantic poets, and to concentrate on concrete, sensory particulars. "It is essential", he said, "to prove that beauty may be in small, dry things."[14] He assumed, however, that the poet reveals a naked reality lying behind conceptual thought; and so, after all, even "small, dry things" in this view become significant. Yet in a poetry of particulars there is certain to be a very fine line between the significant, in this sense, and the merely decorative; it was on the latter side that Read thought the Imagists had mostly remained. All depends on the poet's vision. Read ended his essay with a call to duty:

> Finally, modern England may be "a nest of singing birds", but it is well for us to realize that the poem is still rather a primitive affair, and to make it otherwise there is a call for stern artistic devotion. We must shrink from the exotic and the decadent, and from the sheltered garden of cultivated beauties. Beauty is a discipline, demanding all the intensity of a man's intelligence to present clear and undefiled the infinite quality in things. The artist's vision is the supreme value; the expression of it is the supreme difficulty.
>
> This, then, is the poet's duty and joy: to express the exquisite among his perceptions, achieving so a beauty as definite and indicative as the prints of Hokusai, or the cold grace of immaculate cameos.[15]

Thus the poet's role is serious and his burden heavy. In a form severe, spare, restrained – as coldly and immaculately pure as a cameo or a Japanese woodcut – he must present the 'infinite quality in things'. His vision, in other words, is a mystical insight into reality; it is the 'supreme value', and its expression the 'supreme difficulty'. Read had maintained in his third axiom that expression need only be 'adequate'. Perhaps he meant here, at the end of his essay, that even an 'adequate' expression is a matter of 'supreme difficulty' when one is attempting to express the inexpressible. For Read seems to have been thinking of the poem as an image shorn of all discursive elements, a self-existent object expressive of a knowledge impossible to communicate discursively. It is the symbolist ideal, and not only are there echoes of French symbolist doctrine in Read's theory, but there is in his "immaculate cameos" and "exquisite perceptions" a touch of the preciousness of the English aesthetic movement of the late nineteenth century.

[14] T. E. Hulme, *Speculations* (London, 1924), p. 131.
[15] "Definitions . . .", *loc. cit.*, 78.

2

What Read meant by 'the infinite quality in things' is unclear. It is evident, however, that, whatever it was, it must be attained perceptually, not conceptually. Read, like all the new poets, was determined to eschew abstractions in poetry: the "thing", as Pound claimed, must be treated directly; must be presented, not discussed. "Go in fear of abstractions",[16] Pound had advised the poet. A major shift in poetic taste was taking place. The new poets kept their work close to its basis in concrete, sensory perception; they avoided as anti-poetic everything abstract and ideal. Read, for example, in the course of an essay in *Art and Letters* on the French *unanamiste* school of writers, complained that the poetry of Jules Romains "suffers from the national defect of French poetry. It is conceptual rather than intuitional; it possesses the sophistication of a thought rather than the innocency of a perception."[17] And in an essay on Poe, Read tried to show that, while Poe was important for the modern tradition because he had discovered the 'didactic heresy', and had distinguished Beauty as the only legitimate object of the poem, yet he had been fatally wrong in his notion of what constituted beauty:

The fault of Poe's cannons[sic] lies in their inadequacy – their lack of reach. They are right so far as they cover the field. They discover beauty wherever it exists. They are sufficient to detect the weaknesses of Coleridge and Wordsworth. But in the same breath that Poe praises Tennyson for his lack of earthiness, he can quote as another supreme instance of beauty – "The Bridge of Sighs" ! If only our critic had expended a little of the metaphysical reasoning he deprecated in Coleridge on the pursuit of a logical analysis of the *feeling* he admits to be the true test of poetic worth, he would have discovered – much to his surprise – that the presence of a sense of the Beautiful is curiously concomitant with a quality he would be bound to dub "earthiness." This quality is not an intellectual Truth. But it is a perceptual realism: to make Poe's cannon [sic] complete we must add to qualities ethereal and musical this other cause of that "elevating excitement" which is to Poe and to all of us the revelation of true poetry. Let us affirm once and for all that true inspiration is fed from veins that course through all the flesh of Nature. The instinct of Beauty lives by no other means.[18]

[16] "A Few Don'ts", *loc. cit.*, p. 5.
[17] "An Approach to Jules Romains", *Art and Letters*, II. 1 (1919), 48.
[18] "A Neglected Aspect of Edgar Allan Poe", *Art and Letters*, II. 3 (1919), 141.

Thus Poe's mistake lay in pursuing an unfleshed beauty, an ideal beauty. For Read, a sense of the beautiful involved a 'perceptual realism'; true beauty was beauty fleshed. Poe could be claimed for the modern tradition by virtue of his effort to dismiss from poetry every object but beauty; yet the claim was limited by his failure to tie beauty inextricably to sense.

Beauty, in Read's view of the poetic process, was an emotional response to phenomenal environment, which did not acquire AESTHETIC significance until 'recognized' in an act of vision. From that act it emerged in some mysterious way formed, and was then expressed with appropriate 'decoration'. To acquire aesthetic significance and to acquire form are the same in this view. What seems to happen in the visionary act is that the emotion FINDS an image. In this image it is formed, and there is no content as such. If the poet undertakes to express an IDEA, however, a division between form and content is set up. Read therefore ruled conceptual and discursive elements out of both the poem and the poetic process. The poem is as nontemporal as it is possible for poetry to be: discourse is virtually excluded and the image presented with almost a spatial effect. Similarly, the poetic process in its essential creative act is instantaneous, not discursive; and although the poet needs a 'high philosophic basis' to achieve aesthetic significance, and the act of vision requires what Read calls an 'intellectual selection' among emotions, the poetic process itself remains more emotional than intellectual.

Conceptless and contentless, this poem could well be also meaningless. Read conceded that if the visionary act has been unsuccessful, the poem will have 'emotional significance' only. But he claimed that if the act has been successful, the poem will have 'aesthetic significance' – the poet will be presenting, not simply a 'slice' of his emotions, but "clear and undefiled the infinite quality in things". Thus in the final analysis aesthetic significance is cognitive significance. The poet reveals a kind of knowledge, an insight into the nature of reality. Poetry, then, is a mode of cognition, nondiscursive in its process, and apparently only very tenuously related (if at all) to the discursive mode.

So much we can gather from Read's statements on poetry and the poetic process in his contributions to *Art and Letters*. The further development of his theory of poetry has been a working out of the premises established in these early essays. The study of poetry became for him the study of form. But since he holds that form comes into being through a cognitive process essentially different from the process of discursive thought – consisting as it does in a visionary seizing of images – the study of form became the study of this forming process in the depths of the poet's psyche. The result was a theory combining formalism with expressionism. To study form as it exists in the poem would be to make a technical analysis of effects deliberately wrought, and this Read was not interested in because he did not believe the contriving of these effects to be an essential part of the forming process. His theory, as it developed, could only go in the direction of 'personality', and it is significant that as early as 1919 he had already set his face against the 'impersonal' theory of poetry advanced by Eliot two years earlier. Eliot had contended in his essay, "Tradition and the Individual Talent", that the poet had "not a personality to express, but a particular medium", that poetry is "an escape from personality", and that "*significant* emotion . . . has its life in the poem and not in the history of the poet".[19] Read, in a remark in his essay on Poe, seemed to be replying directly to this contention of Eliot's:

The fault [in Poe's poetry], as the fault of all bad art, lies in the personality of the artist . . . I would be prepared to argue on the other hand that the good of all art is inevitably based on the personality of the artist. In the case of certain poets – Marlowe, Villon, Donne, Blake, for example – if you abstract the expression of their personality you leave a meaningless void.[20]

These contributions to *Art and Letters* leave much to be desired. Despite Read's elaborate 'definitions', one is never very sure of what such terms as 'intelligence', 'beauty', 'form' and the 'aesthetic absolute' really mean. But what we miss most in these writings is a sense of the reality of poetry as it actually exists. Read complained at the beginning of "Definitions . . ." that nowhere "in the criticism of modern poetry, or even in the work of our more conscious poets, can we discern any ideal of poetic form, or any recognition of aesthetic distinctions".[21] Yet in the manifestoes of the Imagists, and in the various writings of Pound, Hulme, F. S. Flint, and

[19] T. S. Eliot, *Selected Essays* (New York, 1932), p. 9.
[20] "A Neglected Aspect . . .", *loc. cit.*, 137.
[21] "Definitions . . .", *loc. cit.*, 73.

others, we feel at least that we are close to poets working out poetic problems; the reality of the poetic medium is always respected. Read, however, in his attempt to set forth an ideal of poetic form worked himself so far away from the poetic medium that it is hard to imagine what a realization of this ideal would be like. He himself could only describe it in a visual analogy – as a cameo, or a Japanese woodcut. Now this tendency to dissolve the poetic medium into something altogether visual is entirely characteristic of Read's theoretical writings. He was a poet himself, and on occasion he discussed practical matters of technique sensibly and perceptively. But as soon as he began to theorize, he tended to be led away from the poem into a nondiscursive realm of visual form. To account for the poem itself seemed always a secondary consideration. The one thing Read was convinced of at the outset was that if the new poetry were to be justified at all, it could only be as a visionary revelation of knowledge, and all questions of the technique of expression were merely peripheral to the central question of the nature of the poet's vision.

Read discussed his early development briefly in his autobiography *Annals of Innocence and Experience*, where he quoted the 'axioms' from his essay, "Definitions towards a Modern Theory of Poetry", and remarked that some of the terms used "are defined with the aid of a psychological jargon which I should now try to avoid; but the essay, differently worded, would still represent my views on the theory of poetry".[22] This is quite true, and perhaps we can with some justice apply to the development of his critical thought a remark he made in the same book about his poetic development:

I think I may say that by the end of the war I had discovered myself and my style – that is to say, I had made an equation between emotion and image, between feeling and expression. So long as I was true to this equation, I need not be afraid of influences or acquired mannerisms... I do not think it will be necessary for a reader of the future to approach my work with squared shoulders: he can accept or reject me on the instant.[23]

So, I believe, it was with Read's critical thought. By the end of the war he had established a theoretical center from which he

[22] *Annals of Innocence and Experience*, p. 98.
[23] *Ibid.*, p. 102.

never deviated. Perhaps no critic was more open to influences, but he never had to be afraid of them because he never allowed them to disturb this center. We can accept or reject his assumptions immediately; we do not have to approach his criticism with "squared shoulders".

II

POETRY AS INTELLIGENCE

1.

By the early 1920's, when Read had begun to establish himself on the critical scene, his writings had assumed a new character. Gone was the mystical aestheticism of his contributions to *Art and Letters*. Read now called himself a 'scientific critic'. He believed criticism, if it were not to lapse into the welter of mere impressionism must become an objective discipline, making full use of scientific knowledge. Gone too was the narrowly aesthetic ideal for poetry of the earlier essays – the preoccupation with 'beauty', and the notion of the poem as an "immaculate cameo", expressing the poet's 'exquisite' perceptions. The poet's vision became now wide and sweeping, taking even metaphysical abstractions for its object. Nevertheless, Read's view of poetry and the poetic process remained fundamentally unchanged: poetry was still a visionary revelation of knowledge and the poetic process an instantaneous act. To defend this view, however, he now probed in every promising scientific and philosophical direction.

The result was bewildering, and no period of Read's development is more difficult to follow than the 1920's. On the one hand, he looked toward science for the means to establish a psychological and even a physiological basis for poetry. On the other hand, he looked toward metaphysics for the means to give poetry a 'sanction' which the methods of natural science could not accord it. It is his search for this sanction which I will trace in this chapter and the next, reserving his investigations into psychoanalysis for later chapters. Actually, as will become evident, the two approaches were only alternative routes to the same end.

The theory Read had outlined in his early work seemed to lead in only one direction: toward a conception of poetry as an intuitional kind of cognition. Thus, if the poet's vision reveals "the infinite quality in things", it penetrates beyond the particulars of sensory experience to a universal. This universal, however, must be something other than the universals of science and philosophy, where unity is attained by connecting particulars discursively. The poet connects them instantaneously: his intuition of unity is a more primary kind of cognition than the scientist's, and in his direct awareness of oneness he ranks with the prophet and the mystic. Such was the conclusion Read arrived at in the late 1920's, but to reach it he went by a surprising route; for in the early 1920's he emerged as an advocate of intellectualism, maintaining that poetry is an intellectual, not an intuitional, mode of apprehension. To trace his progress during the 1920's is, in large part, to trace his shift from a view of poetry as 'intelligence' to a view of it as 'intuition'.

Read's 'intellectualism' is very marked in his first collection of critical essays, *Reason and Romanticism*, and in some of his uncollected contributions to the *Criterion*. His ambition at this time was to unite the scientific and poetic approaches to reality under the sign of 'reason'. He wished to end the conflict between these two modes of apprehension, and he was determined that this should be done without an abandonment of intellect in favor of another cognitive mode, and also without a reduction of the claims of poetry. Although committed to scientific method, he dreaded scientific reductionism. He refused, for example, to accept the kind of justification for poetry advanced by I. A. Richards in *Principles of Literary Criticism*, on the ground that it provided no 'sanction': it made of art, Read said, merely a "mechanical and unrelated harmony of impulses or balance of appetancies".[1] To view poetry, in the manner of Richards, as an emotionally satisfying pseudo-knowledge was, for Read, to denigrate it. He believed that by widening the concept of 'reason' he could provide a 'sanction' without violating the assumptions of scientific materialism. Reason, that is, could include more than discursive ratiocination. "Reason", he said, "should . . . connote the widest evidence of the senses, and of all processes and instincts developed in the long history of man. It is the sum total of awareness ordained and ordered to some specific end or object of attention."[2]

[1] Review of I. A. Richards, *Principles of Literary Criticism, Criterion*, III, 2 (1925), 449.

[2] "Attributes of Criticism", *Reason and Romanticism* (London, 1926), p. 27.

Defined in this way, the term 'reason' could be used to cover both the poetic and the rational modes of apprehension.

Since, however, poetry was for Read a wholly nondiscursive mode, the question of its relation to the discursive or rational mode was acute. As a separate mode, its knowledge would be aesthetic, unique, and nonverifiable; as an arm of the rational mode, its knowledge would be verifiable but no longer unique. All the assumptions of Read's early work pointed to the first of these possibilities; yet, in accordance with his decision to effect unity under the sign of 'reason', it was the second that he adopted: he identified the poetic mode with 'intelligence'. Why Read took this course – why he became an apostle of reason and intelligence, why he aligned himself for a few years with the neo-Thomism of Maritain, with the intellectualism of Julien Benda, with the classicism of Eliot, and with the militant anti-humanism and anti-romanticism of Hulme – has never been clear. From what little Read said about it, one gathers that he regarded this phase of his thought as just another aspect of his romanticism, and in this he was quite right. However, he appeared to take care for some time to keep it out of the permanent body of his critical work. There was too much material from this period that plainly contradicted his mature viewpoint for him to want to display it. He did not deny his past, but neither did he parade it.[3]

[3] *Reason and Romanticism* (London, 1926) and *English Stained Glass* (London, 1926), the two books in which Read's intellectualist position is most noticeable, both remained long out of print. *Reason and Romanticism* was finally reissued (New York, 1963). Read reprinted a number of essays from *Reason and Romanticism* (with some revisions) in *Collected Essays in Literary Criticism* (London, 1938), but excluded others, two of which had a marked intellectualist cast, "The Attributes of Criticism", and "Pure Poetry". Eventually he rewrote "The Attributes of Criticism" for *Poetry and Experience* (London, 1967). During the 1920's Read's contributions to the *Criterion* were frequent, many of them book reviews which remain uncollected. A number of these reflect the same attachment to "order", "control", "reason", and "intellect" that the editor, T. S. Eliot, was promulgating. Read's essay, "Humanism and the Absolute", which reflects Hulme's and Benda's absolutism and antihumanism, after appearing in the *Criterion*, VIII, 31 (1928), was elaborated into a defense of Benda, *Julien Benda and the New Humanism* (Seattle, 1930). This is now again in print as the Introduction to a new edition of Benda's *The Betrayal of the Intellectuals* (Boston, 1955). Read occasionally has attacked his past enthusiasms. In *Poetry and Anarchism* (1938), for example, he deplored Benda's "sterile intellec-

Read's intellectualist position seems to have been in large part a reaction to certain implications of Bergson's ideas. Bergson had held that reality is an inner experience of duration which is only grasped intuitively, whereas intellect, oriented toward action, abstracts and conceptualizes and so distorts this experience. Art, in this view, becomes an intuitive penetration of the flow of reality which lies behind abstractions. Now something of this sort seems to have been Read's assumption in his early work. He had, for example, complained about poetry which is "conceptual rather than intuitional", which "possesses the sophistication of a thought rather than the innocency of a perception". Yet Read's conception of art was always of a vision of reality outside the flow of time, an image static and permanent, whereas Bergson's ideas, as they had been applied to art and literature, had led to an exaltation of the flow of reality in all its subjective and formless immediacy. Read found repellent the notion of a 'rendering' of the flow; he was unimpressed, for example, by both *A la Recherche du temps perdu* and *Ulysses*, finding that "these ambitious renderings of the flow of life ignore the necessity imposed by Henry James on his work, and indulge in the looseness for which he had such an anxious dread".[4] James satisfied Read because of the formal perfection of his novels. His material was 'composed' spatially in the manner of the drama, Read said, rather than 'disposed' temporally in the manner advocated for the novel by a contemporary French literary critic, Albert Thibaudet. Read attributed Thibaudet's theory to the ideas of Bergson, whom he called "merely the latest philosopher of romanticism". The form Read praised in James was in fact the spatial form of a visual art, not the temporal form of a literary medium: "Turn", he said, "to *The Awkward Age* with its carefully placed

---

tualism". He credited Benda with having led him away from Bergson's influence in the post-war years: "This very sharp and subtle mind had first attracted me by an attack on Bergson, at a time when Bergson was very much my enthusiasm. He was not just to Bergson, but he weaned me from my allegiance . . .". (p. 26). Read's comments on the intellectualist phase of his development in *Annals of Innocence and Experience* (pp. 130—133; 106) seem generally to minimize it. For example, one would not realize from his remarks there how strong had been his attachment to neo-Thomist ideas.

[4] "The Modern Novel (Cursory Notes)", *Reason and Romanticism*, p. 217.

'lights', its exacting objectivity, its suggestion of a geometrically contrived quincunx. One cannot resign *that* pleasure, *that* sense of definite pattern, of conscious fidelity to a discipline." "Form", Read said, is "not merely another aspect of style, for it reflects not so much the sensibility as the intelligence of the artist. I would never accuse either Proust or Joyce of a lack of sensibility; but their possession of orderly intelligence . . . is more in doubt."[5] Thus the issue, as it presented itself to Read in the early 1920's, seems to have involved a choice between, on the one hand, the formlessness of pure duration, approached subjectively through intuition, and, on the other hand, the formed, ordered, objective realm of the intellect. Seeing the question in this light, he found himself aligned philosophically with Bergson's opponents, who, against the notion of intuition as the older and more primary mode of apprehension, had contended for intelligence as a single cognitive mode, the source of all order, clarity, and form.[6] It was apparently this association of intelligence with formal order, and of intuition

---

[5] *Ibid.*, p. 218. Read's dissatisfaction with Proust and Joyce was related, I think, to his fundamental bias toward space, rather than time. His sensibility was very strongly visual. This was noted by John Alford in a review of Read's *Icon and Idea* in *Journal of Aesthetics and Art Criticism* XV, 2 (1956), p. 258: "Though Read is himself very conscious of forms and space, he is relatively little concerned with the passage of time. For instance, Gothic architecture as Read sees it is entirely a symbol of remote space, its function as a symbol of events in time is not discussed. This perhaps gives us a clue to Read's basic iconic bias, for the discursive articulation of events is the prime function of language, the aesthetic articulation of time the prime function of music." Of course it can be argued, as it was by Joseph Frank in "Spatial Form in Literature", in *Criticism*, ed. Schorer (New York, 1958), that Proust's method of juxtaposing events and characters, like Eliot's in "The Wasteland" and Pound's in the "Cantos", amounts to a spatializing of time. For Read, however, Proust's work was a monumental "rendering" of time, and not an image outside or above the temporal flow. Read's more recent remarks about Joyce in *Truth is More Sacred* (London, 1961) showed no change in his judgement of him.

[6] See, *e.g.*, Jacques Maritain, *Bergsonian Philosophy and Thomism* (New York, 1954); Wyndham Lewis, *Time and Western Man* (New York, 1927). In the course of a review in the *Criterion*, IV. 3 (1926), 612, Read replied to a charge that the magazine had elevated "form" into a dogma, and concluded with this remark: "A significant mind is only significant by virtue of its organisation, and the intellect is the only organising faculty known to man. It is the only ultimate measure of values, and values are the only end of criticism."

with the flux of duration, that lay behind Read's notion of poetry as an intellectual mode of apprehension.

His criterion for poetry, which in 1918 had been "the quality of the vision", was now stated in considerably different terms:

"What, then, *is* your criterion?" someone might ask. It is the quality of intelligence inherent in the poem. "But what is intelligence?" might be the further query. It is the same faculty of "direct apprehension" already distinguished by medieval philosophy, and since then somewhat compromised, in differing degrees, by Descartes, Spinoza, and Bergson. It is dangerous perhaps to describe it as a "faculty," for it is in reality but one aspect of the single faculty of apprehension. It is perhaps only the distinction between reason which is concentrated on a single object and reason which is discursive. It is a distinction clearly and for all time made by no less an authority than St. Thomas Aquinas: "intelligere enim est simpliciter veritatem intelligibilem apprehendere: ratiocinari autem est procedere de uno intellecto ad aluid, ad veritatem intelligibilem cognoscendam ..."[7]

Read explained this distinction no further. The consequence of it is, however, that the poetic mode becomes identical with that act of the mind which in the scholastic and classical philosophy is the simple apprehension of intelligible truth. It is, in other words, the act of understanding rather than reasoning, or what St. Thomas called 'intellect' in distinction from 'reason'. In man, this is the simple understanding of first principles from which reasoning begins and to which it returns, but in angels, who have no need for discursive reason, it is the sole mode of apprehension. The poetic intelligence, then, is distinguished from the discursive reason, but only, as Read said, in that they are both aspects of a single faculty – or as St. Thomas said "By the same power do we understand and reason: and so it is clear that in man reason and intellect are the same power."[8] Now the Thomist's simple

---

[7] "Pure Poetry", *Reason and Romanticism*, p. 66.

[8] *The "Summa Theologica" of St. Thomas Aquinas*, Part I, tr. Fathers of the English Dominican Province (London, n. d.), p. 110. St. Thomas was arguing the question, "Whether the Reason is Distinct from the Intellect?" The translation of a part of his answer is as follows: "Reason and intellect in man cannot be distinct powers. We shall understand this clearly if we consider their respective actions. For to understand is simply to apprehend intelligible truth: and to reason is to advance from one thing understood to another, so as to know an intelligible truth. And therefore angels who, according to their nature, possess perfect knowledge of intelligible truth,

apprehension of intelligible truth can, of course, also be called 'intuition' and is sometimes so translated, but it is essentially different from Bergsonian intuition. For to Bergson, who stressed the inward experience of duration and the inability of the conceptualizing intellect to grasp this experience, intuition was the primary mode of apprehension. But to the Thomists, intuition is simply the beginning of the inherently discursive process through which man comes to know an objective reality. If the scholastic distinction has been "compromised", as Read claimed, it has been by changing it from a distinction within the intelligence to a distinction between the intelligence and some more subjective mode of apprehension. Read was attempting to keep the poetic vision as a non-discursive mode of apprehension, but to place it within the intelligence, where it could function as an intellectual power.[9]

2

To see how, in the early 1920's, Read conceived the poetic mode to function in relation to the rational, it is necessary to examine

---

have no need to advance from one thing to another; but apprehend the truth simply and without mental discussion ... But man arrives at the knowledge of intelligible truth by advancing from one thing to another; and therefore he is called rational. Reasoning, therefore, is compared to understanding, as movement is to rest, or acquisition to possession; of which one belongs to the perfect, the other to the imperfect."

[9] For a time during the 1920's Read appeared to be a convinced Thomist. For example, in *English Stained Glass*, p. 22, he remarked that Thomism was "the definite constitution of modern philosophy, and it may be doubted if all departures from the essence of this philosophy – and particularly the subjectivist philosophy initiated by Descartes and established by Kant – have been other than unfortunate aberrations of the human reason." And in the course of a review of Count Hermann Keyserling's *Travel Diary of a Philosopher* in the *Criterion*, IV, 1 (1926), 192, he contrasted the "loose subjectivism" of Keyserling with the thought of St. Thomas, and remarked: "Significantly enough, Keyserling never once mentions the name of Rousseau. For these precious 'souls' are jealous of their exemplars, and would not willingly admit that they appear from time to time *as a type*, whose only effect is to cloud for a while the clear stream of thought ... It is perhaps the seeming hopelessness of our opposition that adds bitterness to these observations on Keyserling's book. A revival of the scholastic attitude seems very remote, especially in England ..."

his essay, "The Nature of Metaphysical Poetry". Read contended in this essay that conceptual thought could be a legitimate object of the poetic vision without in any way changing the nature of that vision. The poem, that is, would presumably remain essentially an image, but fused into this image could be the abstractions of thought. This was a departure from his early view that poetry was based only on an emotional response to phenomena; it might, he now held, be also based on an emotional response to conceptual abstractions. The two types of poetry Read designated as 'lyrical' and 'metaphysical', and he attempted to ground them in a distinction between the 'content' of emotions: concrete emotions are expressed in the lyric, and abstract emotions in metaphysical poetry. The lyric is a poem which "in its purest state is concerned with the direct awareness of phenomenal environment". Metaphysical poetry he defined as "the emotional apprehension of thought". It is the emotion, however, that makes it poetry, not the thought:

While metaphysical poetry always exists in association with a mind that is didactic, insomuch as its life is a life of thought, yet it derives its poetic quality from another source, which is emotional. As an illustration we might represent thought and emotion as two separately revolving pulleys: one, emotion, has a revolution a thousand times greater than the other; but by the operation of a lever the two pulleys are connected, and immediately thought is accelerated to the speed or intensity of emotion.[10]

This means, apparently, that at the moment of poetic creation, thought ceases to be discursive: it remains thought, but it takes on characteristics that are essentially non-temporal – "the speed or intensity of emotion". Read's pulley illustration is perhaps not entirely successful here, but I think his intention was to emphasize the paradoxicalness of metaphysical poetry. For such poetry, from his standpoint, must involve a nondiscursive apprehension of discursive thought in which the latter is transformed. Read pointed out that discursive thought cannot be made 'poetical' merely by casting it into a poetic form, and that Milton stands as the great example of a poet who failed to understand this: "Milton did not think poetically, but merely expounded thought

[10] "The Nature of Metaphysical Poetry", *Reason and Romanticism*, p. 38. First published in the *Criterion*, I, 3 (1923).

in verse; psychologically he was conscious all the time of a dualism – on the one side the thought to be expounded, on the other side the poetic mould into which his thought had to be smelted. The true metaphysical poet is conscious of no such dualism: his thought is in its very process poetical."[11]

We are naturally reminded here of Eliot, who also regarded Milton as an example to be avoided, and who two years earlier had described metaphysical poetry as the "direct, sensuous apprehension of thought".[12] Perhaps Read's essay does represent a coming-to-terms with Eliot's poetic ideal – an ideal considerably more sophisticated than the one Read had started with. For Eliot had tried to achieve, not a beauty like the "cold grace of immaculate cameos", from which thought and passion were debarred, but a fusion of thought and passion, best exemplified in certain English poets of the seventeenth century and best described by the term 'wit'. But Read's aim was fundamentally different from Eliot's, despite the similarity of his definition of metaphysical poetry. For Eliot had been interested chiefly in the technique of the English metaphysical school and in the possibility of using it to express the variety and disparity of his own age. "It appears likely", he had said,

that poets in our civilization, as it exists at present, must be *difficult*. Our civilization comprehends great variety and complexity, and this variety and complexity, playing upon a refined sensibility, must produce various and complex results. The poet must become more and more comprehensive, more allusive, more indirect, in order to force, to dislocate if necessary, language into his meaning ... Hence we get something which looks very much like the conceit – we get, in fact, a method curiously similar to that of the "metaphysical poets", similar also in its use of obscure words and of simple phrasing.[13]

Eliot did not apparently believe that the modern poet could attempt, through poetry, to bring an end to the dissociation of the modern mind. For Eliot, unity would presumably have to come from outside poetry, if it came at all. The point of Read's essay, however, was precisely that the modern poet could presume to unify POETICALLY the modern mind. Metaphysical poetry was for him not a seventeenth century technique which might be useful to the modern poet, but

[11] *Ibid.*, p. 52.
[12] T. S. Eliot, "The Metaphysical Poets", *Selected Essays* (New York, 1932), p. 246. First published in 1921.
[13] *Ibid.*, p. 248.

a kind of poetry, neglected of late, which might heal the dissociation of the contemporary mind. Read was not, in fact, greatly interested in the English metaphysicals, except for Donne. "Very few", he said, "were metaphysical in any sense", most of their poetry being actually lyrical: "a metaphysical metaphor or concept is included in a poem predominantly lyrical in mood".[14] It was rather to Dante that Read turned for his point of contrast with the dissociation of modern poetry. He found in Dante a "bold interfusion of thought and actuality" in which lay "the whole meaning of metaphysical poetry". And it seemed to be the presence of this "interfusion", rather than of any particular technique, that decided whether a poet belonged to Read's metaphysical tradition. His tradition began with Lucretius, included Dante and Calvacanti, Donne and Chapman, and ended with Wordsworth. Nothing exemplifies better his difference from Eliot than his inclusion of Wordsworth in the metaphysical tradition. Indeed, Read himself seemed a little embarrassed by Wordsworth's technique. Remarking of some lines from "The Recluse" that "I might go a long way to find a better example of metaphysical poetry", he went on to admit that the passage "comes dangerously near to being rhetorical". "But rhetoric", he added, "is only reprehensible when it is hollow, as it mostly is; when it is compact with thought, as this rhetoric of Wordsworth's is, it is powerful beyond any other mode of expression".[15] What bothered Read, of course, was Wordsworth's discursiveness. Yet there is undeniably present in Wordsworth's poetry an "emotional apprehension of thought" and an "interfusion of thought and actuality". Furthermore, Wordsworth's work can be seen as an attempt to heal, synthesize, and restore – an attempt to recover a unified outlook amid the changing conditions of thought. And this was exactly the mission Read assigned to the modern poet. He concluded his essay by considering "the possibility of recovering this lost tradition" which had come to a temporary end with Wordsworth.

A new metaphysical poetry, Read made clear, was not to be a reversion to outworn modes from which modern poets had revolted. He emphasized that in his definition, 'emotional apprehension of thought', the word 'apprehension' implied a "degree of

---

[14] "The Nature of Metaphysical Poetry", loc. cit., p. 40.
[15] Ibid., pp. 53-54.

economy" and a "corresponding intensity", and that "emotional apprehension should appear as a fairly 'hard', even as a necessarily 'dry' process".[16] The words "hard" and "dry" here come from Imagist doctrine, being catch words used by T. E. Hulme to describe the new poetry. A contemporary metaphysical poetry, then, was to have the characteristics of the new poetry but to be based on an emotional response to intellectual abstractions rather than to the phenomenal environment. As to what these abstractions might be in the present age, Read suggested the work of the physicists:

However pitiful our social life may be, yet there does exist an intelligent minority of considerable vigour and positive achievement: I refer particularly to the modern physicists, whose work would seem to provide a whole system of thought and imagery ready for fertilization in the mind of the poet. For, if the assumptions of this essay are accepted, it will be seen that science and poetry have but one ideal, which is the satisfaction of the reason. Aesthetic satisfaction is not, as is too often assumed, the satisfaction of the senses (the senses are never satisfied), but *is* the satisfaction of the co-ordinating judgment of the intellect – in symmetry, in rhythm, and in all the properties of universal truth . . . The scientific ideal does at any rate carry us into the full stream of all that is valuable in our age. Science has established a large number of "phenomena", but these phenomena remain discreet. They lack harmonic unity. Perhaps mathematical philosophy is working in one direction to establish this unity; metaphysical poetry, working in a different direction, can, without presumption, aim to the same end.[17]

Thus Read proposed that the modern poet work hand in hand with the mathematical philosopher to unify the contemporary mind. The poet could approach this great task from his own direction with as much right as the physicist from his, and the poetic unity achieved would be as valid as the mathematical. In Read's view, such a contemporary metaphysical poetry would be in contact with the whole tradition of metaphysical poetry because it would be simply another aspect of the quest for universals. Metaphysical poetry, he said, is "but the precise statement of such abstractions as the poet derives from his experience. Perhaps, in the scholastic sense, it is the poetry of universals."[18] The contemporary poet, then, by working toward a 'harmonic unity' of discrete phenomena,

[16] *Ibid.*, p. 55.
[17] *Ibid.*, pp. 57—58.
[18] *Ibid.*, p. 56.

would be writing, in the scholastic sense, a poetry of universals, even as Dante did.

The difficulty with this view, however, is that where Dante was dealing with a unity discursively ascertained through metaphysical analysis and already elaborated in language, the modern metaphysical poet must emotionally apprehend abstractions which cannot even be stated discursively except in mathematical symbols. The unity he creates must be the result of an intuition of harmony which represents probably a deeper interfusion of mind and nature than even Wordsworth contemplated. In the Thomistic distinction between 'reason' and 'intellect', which Read had adopted, 'intellect' operates in conjunction with 'reason'; as a separate mode it is not found in human apprehension, only in angelic. In Read's notion of poetry, however, it is difficult to see how this mode of 'direct apprehension' can be considered intellectual in the Thomistic sense; it seems more like Bergson's 'intuition' than St. Thomas's 'intellect'. For behind it lies the same assumption Bergson made – that the abstracting, conceptualizing intellect represents only a partial mode of cognition; to achieve unity another mode is required – subjective, intuitive, poetic. These two modes may be arbitrarily yoked under the sign of 'reason', as here done by Read, but they nevertheless remain different things practiced by different people, the scientist and the poet. To say that their ends are the same – "the satisfaction of the reason" – is only to claim that they are both cognitive; but since they differ so widely in their operation, it would seem more logical to give them different names. Read, however, refused to do this, and the result was the paradox we meet repeatedly in his work of the 1920's: art is proclaimed to be an intellectual mode of apprehension, but when we examine its operation we cannot find anything intellectual about it.

III

POETRY AS INTUITION

1

Read's position in the early 1920's was not an intellectualist position, even though he had aligned himself with the intellectualists. He was not, like Maritain, for example, holding up the discursive intelligence of the classical and scholastic tradition as the one great cognitive principle. But neither was he, like Richards, claiming that the referential thought of the scientist is the only kind that yields genuine knowledge. Art was for Read an alternative approach to reality, and as such it was a mode of apprehension in its own right. This was not always apparent, however, and in the critical wars of the 1920's between the advocates of 'intuition' and the advocates of 'intelligence', Read seemed to be carrying the banner of 'intelligence' with great boldness and resolution.

We can see how the critical lines were drawn in this matter from a debate in the *Criterion* that followed Eliot's review of Read's *Reason and Romanticism*. An anonymous reviewer in the *Times* (Middleton Murry) had challenged Read's "narrow, scholastic" use of the word 'intelligence', contending that the "faculty or act of simple apprehension of truth" should be called 'intuition' rather than 'intelligence'.[1] Eliot noted with some asperity this remark in his own review: " . . . we only complicate our ignorance by calling it 'intuition,' and . . . for anyone who has devoted even a little attention to St. Thomas, or to Aristotle, the term 'intelligence' is adequate . . . . To insist on another faculty 'intuition' is merely to demand a more potent and thuriferous ju-ju".[2] In June, 1927, an article by Middleton Murry called "Towards a Synthesis"

---

[1] "Reason and Criticism", *Times Literary Supplement* (July 8, 1926), 454. Reprinted in Middleton Murry's *Countries of the Mind* (Oxford, 1931).

[2] T. S. Eliot, review of *Reason and Romanticism, Criterion*, IV, 4 (1926), 757.

appeared in the *Criterion* as an answer to this statement of Eliot's. It was in turn challenged in articles by M. C. D'Arcy, Charles Mauron, Ramon Fernandez, and Eliot, and finally, in December, 1927, Murry had the last word. Despite numerous interesting digressions, the central issue in the long debate was quite clear: is intuition a mode of cognition separate from the intelligence? On this issue the writers lined up, with Murry on the side of 'intuition' as a distinctive mode, and the others, in varying degrees, on the side of 'intelligence' as comprehensive. Murry believed intuition to be something other than – and perhaps even opposed to – the intelligence. He claimed there is a mode of apprehending reality which is not a part of the intelligence but which does not altogether rule it out. Art, he thought, is the most obvious example of this.[3] Eliot, however, denied the 'truth' of aesthetic intuitions as such, and accused Murry of opposing intelligence, worshipping 'intuition' and the 'time spirit' of Bergson, and trying to substitute art for religion.[4] Father D'Arcy, also, would not allow another mode of cognition outside the intelligence and pointed out that art employs other activities of the soul than philosophy: the artist "creates" or "makes", while the philosopher "discovers", or attempts to "know".[5]

Read took no part in this debate, although it had been his designation of 'intelligence' as the criterion for poetry which had really started the whole thing. The views he had expressed in *Reason and Romanticism*, however, were sternly opposed to the notion of a cognitive mode outside the intelligence. He engaged, for example, in a scornful rebuttal of the American critic, Waldo Frank, who, Read said, had proposed abandoning the traditional approach to truth through the intellect and adopting in its place a "new language" of art. For Read it was "mere superstition to imagine that what cannot be known in the mind and by intellectual symbols may be apprehended in some other indefinite way. It

[3] J. Middleton Murry, "Concerning Intelligence", *Criterion*, VI, 6 (1927), 528.

[4] T. S. Eliot, "Mr. Middleton Murry's Synthesis", *Criterion*, VI, 4 (1927), 342. "Intuition", Eliot remarked, "must have its place in a world of discourse; there may be room for intuitions both at the top and the bottom, or at the beginning and the end; but that intuition must always be tested, and capable of test, in a whole of experience in which intellect plays a large part."

[5] M. C. D'Arcy, S. J., "The Thomistic Synthesis and Intelligence", *Criterion*, VI, 3 (1927), 220.

is mysticism in its most illogical form – mysticism which pretends to be, not merely an alternative to scientific truth (and therefore under certain conditions an acceptable mysticism), but something more inclusive of reality than the scientific method."[6] Instead of Frank's "conquest of . . . new forms of life by the instrumentality of an unimaginable art", Read said that he preferred to believe in "an art which is the incorporation and enlightening of the ground gained by the intelligence. The critical spirit is not essentially negative or destructive; it can co-exist with the creative spirit . . . Art is not an invention in vacuo; it is rather a selection from chaos, a definition from the amorphous, a concretion within the 'terrible fluidity' of life . . . It would be better to sacrifice art altogether than to make it a mere anomalous groping into the void of Nescience."[7] Against Frank's "new creed, of which Art is the ineffable Logos", Read hurled Thomism, the "most significant half", he said, of Western thought. "If we were required to point to a philosophy worked out in the terms of Western reality and consonant with our deepest instincts, we should turn to medieval philosophy and particularly to the thought of St. Thomas Aquinas." The other half of Western thought, he said, was that 'subjectivist trend' which "sees the East through rose-coloured spectacles". "Let us recall Schopenhauer's claim on behalf of his master: 'It was reserved for Kant to carry victoriously into Europe and its philosophy that profound idealistic vision common to all Asia . . .'"[8] In place of this subjectivism, Read proposed the intellectual clarity and order advocated by the French critic, Henri Massis, who had observed, "Le caractère de l'Occident, c'est la *distinction*." For Massis, Read said, this characteristic of Western thought was summed up in "la sentence classique d'Anaxagore: 'Au début tout était confondu; l'intelligence vint et mît chaque chose en ordre'."[9] From the solidity of this classical position, then, in which intellect appears as the great ORDERING faculty, Read could afford to be patronizing:

In a way I regret having to controvert, even to this extent, Mr. Frank's position; it is so urgent, so fearless, so straightforward. But it would lead ultimately, I think, to untenable superstitions and a nebulous art.

[6] "Attributes of Criticism", *loc. cit.*, p. 18.

[7] *Ibid.*, pp. 21—22.

[8] *Ibid.*, pp. 12—13.

[9] *Ibid.*, p. 13.

The critical spirit has gained so much after all these years, in clarity, precision, truth itself, that it is a pity to go back on it merely because it has left us, for the present, in such a naked condition of misery and chaos. We need to create a new unity, or perhaps to recover an old one. But if the critical spirit cannot give us this, no other force will, for that spirit is the highest and most perfected function in man.[10]

Read thus committed himself to pursue unity through intelligence – the 'critical spirit' – the only force he considered capable of attaining it. He looked backward to the 'old' unity of the Thomistic synthesis, and at the same time forward to a 'new' unity, based on contemporary modes of thought, which he hoped might do for the modern mind what St. Thomas had done for the medieval mind.

Read did not reprint the essay in which this declaration for 'intelligence' appeared until he rewrote it in 1967, and indeed its original version makes strange reading in the light of his later opinions. For not only did he subsequently establish himself in that 'subjectivist trend' of Western thought which he here deplored, but he came to see the aesthetic faculty as existing prior to the intellectual and functioning as the chief agency in the evolution of human consciousness. Far from believing that it is "mere superstition to imagine that what cannot be known in the mind and by intellectual symbols may be apprehended in some other indefinite way", he held finally that intellectual symbols can only express that which is already aesthetically realized. "We manipulate ideas by logic or scientific method, but we come upon them in the contemplation of images", he said.[11] In 1926, however, he was willing to concede to art at best only an alternative, not a prior, role in cognition. Even so, this alternative role amounted in practice to a subjective and virtually independent mode of cognition. For all Read's strictures against Waldo Frank's attempt to make of art a 'new language', he too was trying to do the same thing, except that he was not willing to abandon the 'other language' of science.

[10] *Ibid.*, p. 20.

[11] *Icon and Idea* (Cambridge, Mass., 1955), p. 6. *Cf. Art and the Evolution of Man* (London, 1951); *The Forms of Things Unknown* (London, 1960).

2

From a philosophical standpoint, the choice confronting Read between 'intelligence' and 'intuition' was real enough, and he could argue eloquently for 'intelligence'. But his view of art as a non-discursive cognitive mode could be made to fit in with these arguments only by arbitrarily declaring this mode to be intellectual. The result was unconvincing. Given Read's view of the poetic process, unity was not going to be attained by assimilating the poetic mode to 'reason'; much more likely would be an assimilation of 'reason' to the poetic mode, and there is evidence that he had begun such a development almost as soon as *Reason and Romanticism* was published. Indeed, it is tempting to speculate that Read stayed out of the 'intuition-intelligence' debate in the *Criterion* because he found himself in greater agreement with Middleton Murry's side of the argument than with Eliot's. Murry's *Times* review of *Reason and Romanticism* (which sparked the debate) had been a remarkably perceptive article which culminated in an outline of that 'organic' philosophy to which Read soon turned: the 'order of great art' is not 'intellectual', Murry said, but 'organic', a higher order under which the intelligence itself is subsumed.[12]

The appearance of Whitehead's *Science and the Modern World* in 1925 marked, I believe, the beginning of the end for Read's intellectualist phase. Whitehead's earlier books had already impressed him. He said in *Annals of Innocence and Experience*, for example, that Whitehead's *Principles of Natural Knowledge* (1922) had strengthened his conviction "that a profound relation exists between the reality of art and the reality of nature". He said he noted that certain passages in this book, particularly those in which Whitehead indentifies 'rhythm' with life, "might, without any violence, be transposed from a work on physics to one on aesthetics".[13] It was in *Science and the Modern World*, however, that Read found a doctrine of intuition which he could use to give poetry the kind of "sanction' he had been looking for.

Read reviewed *Science and the Modern World* for the *Criterion*, and the impression it had made on him can be seen from his opening statement: "This is perhaps the most important book published in

---

[12] "Reason and Criticism", *loc. cit.*, 454.
[13] *Annals of Innocence and Experience*, p. 227.

the conjoint realms of science and philosophy since Descartes'
Discourse on Method: at least, it is the first attempt to issue out
of a certain way of thought which has prevailed since Descartes'
day. It embodies the material of a revolution in our whole concept
of life or being, and seeks to reinterpret, not only categories of
science and philosophy, but even those of religion and art."[14]
Read felt that Whitehead was working toward a unification of
modern thought on the basis of mathematical physics, even as
Aquinas had unified medieval thought on the basis of Aristotelian
science. He compared Whitehead to St. Thomas because he
"reunites once more . . . the procedures of science and philosophy . .
identifying the nature of structure and value".[15]

Read believed Whitehead was putting back together what
Descartes had taken apart: mind and matter. The separation of
these had led, according to Whitehead, to private worlds of morals
and experience on the one hand, and to the valuelessness of mechanical matter on the other. This separation, Read said, meant destruc-
tion for art. Whitehead's insistence on "the evidence of poetry"
particularly impressed him. He said Whitehead "believes that the
ultimate appeal is to naive experience; and he correlates the world
of thought with the world of sense".[16]

Now Whitehead's view of intellect is much like Bergson's. He
correlates the worlds of 'thought' and 'sense' on the basis of his
philosophy of 'organism', in which reality is 'process' and intellectual
distinctions are abstractions from 'process'. In appealing to 'naive
experience', Whitehead appeals to an awareness, for the most
part below the level of conscious discrimination, of 'dim and massive'
aesthetic relationships. In this way he seeks to end the Cartesian
bifurcation of nature. His final recourse is to intuition, and, as
with Bergson, some of his evidence comes from poetry and
art.[17]

---

[14] Review of *Science and the Modern World, Criterion,* IV, 3 (1926), 581.
[15] *Ibid.,* 582.
[16] *Ibid.,* 581.
[17] See – in addition to *Science and the Modern World* – *Adventures of
Ideas* (New York, 1933), and *Modes of Thought* (New York, 1938) for these
aspects of Whitehead's thought. After studying Whitehead, Read's view
of St. Thomas seems to have changed. In a review of Henry Bett's *Johannes
Scotus Erigena, Criterion,* IV, 4 (1926), 780—782, he found Erigena's scholastic philosophy easier to reconcile with organicist thought than St. Thomas's. He said that Erigena attained "a monistic doctrine by the assump-

A few months after his review of *Science and the Modern World*, Read published an essay, "The Dethronement of Descartes", in which he worked out a kind of ultimate justification, or 'sanction', for poetry, based on Whitehead's ideas, to which he has clung ever since.[18] In this essay Read brought together Maritain and Whitehead, two contemporary philosophers of opposed views who nevertheless joined in rejecting the Cartesian separation of mind and matter. Maritain represented the Thomistic synthesis. His score against Descartes, Read explained, was that he had rejected "the essentially discursive nature of human reasoning"; Descartes had "conceived human thought as of the type of angelic thought"; he had made "thought independent of things – intuitive as to its mode, innate as to its origin, autonomous as to its nature".[19]

Read's objection, however, was not to Descartes's method as such. He believed this method had failed, "not from any inherent fallacy, but because it was compelled to operate in a dualistic universe. A mind quite independent of the objects of the senses

---

tion that the dualism of the universe is not the real opposition of equally real principles, but the apparent duality of one principle, as seen from above and from below . . .". Diversity and unity are thus two aspects of the same thing. Things appear diverse because of the finitude of our minds. "Such an intellectual interpretation bears a very sympathetic relation to such philosophy as has been elaborated by modern science – above all to the philosophy of Professor Whitehead . . .". Erigena's notion of a 'creative godhead' meant that creation was necessary, its act or process 'grounded' in the essence of God; whereas for Aquinas there was only an act of the will of God, no necessity. Erigena's conception, then, is of a more 'organic' connection between the Creator and the creation. "In this matter our sympathy should go out to Erigena rather than to Aquinas, for the result of modern science has been to make an organic conception of the universe absolutely essential, a conception in which there is perhaps room for certain destructive aspects of change (metabolism), but in which the fundamental energy is creative."

[18] *Times Literary Supplement*, Sep. 9, 1926, 585—586. This essay was retitled "Descartes" and included in *The Sense of Glory* (London, 1929), and later reprinted in *Collected Essays in Literary Criticism*. My quotations are from *The Sense of Glory*. The notion of intuition set forth here has remained fundamental for Read. He remarked, for example, in *Art and Industry*, 3rd ed. (London, 1953), p. 31: "I have tried to reach a satisfactory definition of it [intuition] for general critical purposes in an essay on 'Descartes' . . .".

[19] "Descartes", *loc. cit.*, p. 66.

could only know itself."[20] Read found Cartesianism "non-poetic in a very profound sense", for it involved the "break-up of all values that cannot be proved within the strictly private world of psychological experience". Under this conception, "beauty can only be a mechanical harmony, devoid of spiritual animation, deficient in the sense of glory".[21] Examining Cartesian intuition, he found it very likely to be deceptive, since, he said, "we now realize" that the mind has "certain fixed states of belief which have little to do with the understanding" and are probably "unconscious rationalizations of personal experience".[22]

Thus Read was not bothered by Descartes's rejection of "the essentially discursive nature of human reasoning". He said, in fact, that "the difference between discursive and intuitive reasoning, which M. Maritain would make a difference between human and angelic nature, is only a temporal difference".[23] What Read objected to was the fact that Cartesian intuition is cut off from the world or things and may be affected by 'unconscious rationalizations'. He did not consider, however, the assumption behind Maritain's statement: that the "essentially discursive nature of human reasoning" is precisely what binds the mind to the world of things, and that Cartesian intuition differed from this in more than merely a temporal sense, since its effect was to separate the mind from that world; it was, in Maritain's scholastic terminology, "of the type of angelic thought".

Read's definition of intuition sought to improve on the Cartesian theory by "limiting the sense of the process to objective apprehension, and this, in its turn, means identifying intuition with the poetic process. For poetry is the apprehension or verbalization of an objective world . . . Perception is of things, not of abstractions, and intuition is a perceptive process – the only process that perceives things in nakedness rather than in a cloak of secondhand words."[24] Thus, as 'objective apprehension', intuition would be tied to the world of things and presumably not subject to distortion by unconscious rationalization. The implication here is that reality lies behind abstractions and is apprehended in its 'nakedness' only

[20] *Ibid.*, p. 74.
[21] *Ibid.*, p. 72.
[22] *Ibid.*, p. 74.
[23] *Ibid.*, p. 66.
[24] *Ibid.*, p. 75.

intuitively. But Read proceeded to connect this essentially Bergsonian idea with Whitehead's conception of 'pattern' and 'value.'
He said that "it may be doubted whether intuition can stop at
particular things. Its range is not only immediate, but also universal." He quoted Whitehead's statement: "We have to admit that
the body is the organism whose states regulate our cognisance
of the world. The unity of the perceptual field therefore must be
a unity of bodily experience. In being aware of the bodily experience, we must thereby be aware of aspects of the whole spatio-
temporal world as mirrored within the bodily life." Furthermore,
Whitehead had said, as Read quoted him, that "an individual
entity, whose own life-history is a part within the life-history of
some larger, deeper, more complete pattern, is liable to have aspects
of that larger pattern reflected in its own being".[25] Read said,

This new concept of pattern is very suggestive for a possible theory
of intuition. Pattern is an event evolved in time. It is spatially "now",
but only by virtue of its endurance over a definite lapse of time. To
express the same idea inversely, "endurance is the repetition of the
pattern in successive events." And "pattern" must in some way be
correlated with "value". Value is the outcome of limitation. It is the
definition of the particular pattern. It constitutes the intrinsic reality
of an event. We may visualize an object with "an unclouded and atten-
tive mind". Such is perception. We may discover relations between
the visual images thus provided. That is the faculty of imagination;
in poetry it is the invention of metaphors. There is then a further process
and a higher faculty, and there is at present no better way of describing
it than by saying that it is the sudden perception of a pattern in life:
the sudden realization of the fact that an organic event, of which we
are a part, is in its turn the part of a greater unity, of a unity limited
in time and space, formal and harmonious. This further perception or
realization is the process to which we might perhaps limit the term
"intuition"; and it is, under the aspect of expression, the process of
poetry. In this way poetry involves everything: it is the sense of integral
unity without which, not only no poetry, but no philosophy – even no
religion – is ever possible.[26]

Beginning, then, with a perception of particulars lying in their
'nakedness' behind abstractions, Read's intuitive process extends,
through an awareness of the 'bodily experience' which in turn
mirrors "aspects of the whole spatio-temporal world", to a percep-

[25] *Ibid.*, p. 76.
[26] *Ibid.*, pp. 76 – 77.

tion of a universal 'pattern'. This pattern is 'formal and harmonious' and its value is its 'definition', the outcome of its 'limitation'. The original perception apparently acts like a pebble thrown into a pond: concentric ripples from its splash widen across the surface until they lose themselves on the shore of a 'greater unity'. Furthermore, poetry IS this intuitive process, and therefore "poetry involves everything".[27] Poetry is thus identified with the apprehension of unity which underlies all science, philosophy, and even religion. Poetry is at last 'sanctioned'.

This is the ultimate justification for poetry as cognition, because it gives to the discursive mode the function merely of elaborating intuitions which are essentially poetic. As in Shelley's *Defense of Poetry*, the poets become the "unacknowledged legislators of mankind". But where Shelley, the nineteenth-century romanticist, held that the poet's vision stripped the veil of familiarity from the world and penetrated to a realm of absolute IDEAS, Read, the twentieth-century romanticist, gave all conceptual discourse over to the scientist and philosopher. The 'veil of familiarity' that his poet strips from the world is a conceptual veil, and the realm to which his vision penetrates is an aesthetic realm of "pattern". By avoiding abstractions, the poet attains the most fundamental unity of all. Read's poet was "dragging in the infinite" quite as much as any nineteenth-century romantic poet, but he was pulling it from underneath.

3

If we view Read's progress in the 1920's from the standpoint of the philosophical systems he embraced, it appears that he shifted in the short space of three or four years from the Aristotelian-Thomistic synthesis to the Whiteheadian organic synthesis – – from, that is, what he called the 'old' unity to the 'new'. This is true enough, but it is misleading to conclude that he embraced these systems as anything but useful philosophical tools. His allegiance was not to any intellectual synthesis, but simply to poetry, which he was determined to justify as a mode of apprehension. Any philosophy which would buttress this claim in an age

[27] This statement as it originally appeared in *Times Literary Supplement* was even stronger: "And in this way poetry is everything . . .".

of scientific reductionism was useful to him. The problem was to establish poetry as a cognitive mode by the most convincing means, and to conceive it as 'intelligence' proved less convincing than to conceive it as 'intuition'. The nature of the poetic mode, however, remained exactly the same, whether Read described it as an intellectual 'direct apprehension', or as an intuitive 'sudden realization' of 'pattern': in either case it was immediate and nondiscursive. What changed was the way he defined its relation to the rational mode.

It must be emphasized, however, that in adopting a Whiteheadian doctrine of intuition, Read was not aiming to undermine intelligence. He has never felt it necessary to abandon intellect in favor of another mode, because he has always maintained that intellect, too, in its most essential aspect is nondiscursive. This was equally true whether he conceived poetry as an intellectual or an intuitional mode. The distinction between 'intelligence' and 'intuition' is, in fact, really beside the point, for Read's poetic mode encompasses 'intelligence' and 'thought' and 'reason', so long as these are understood to be nondiscursive. There is only one point he could never concede, and that was the one raised by Maritain: "the essentially discursive nature of human reasoning".

Read's aim remained to bring 'science' and 'poetry' together, but soon after the mid-1920's he abandoned the attempt to do this under the sign of 'reason': poetry, by being identified with intuition, had come to have priority over the rational mode, and thus unity was attained only at the expense of 'reason'. His essay on metaphysical poetry, in which he had attempted to show how the two modes could be brought together in the poem, therefore required some revision when he included it in his *Collected Essays in Literary Criticism* in 1938. The statement, " . . . science and poetry have but one ideal, which is the satisfaction of the reason", he changed by adding the word "metaphysical" before the word "poetry",[28] thus making it refer only to a particular kind of poetry; whereas he had originally meant poetry itself, as a cognitive mode. And the sentence following this he dropped altogether:

[28] "The Nature of Metaphysical Poetry", *Collected Essays in Literary Criticism* (London, 1938), p. 87.

Aesthetic satisfaction is not, as is too often assumed, the satisfaction of the senses (the senses are never satisfied), but *is* the satisfaction of the co-ordinating judgement of the intellect – in symmetry, in rhythm, and in all the properties of universal truth.

With a few other, less substantive, changes the essay fits in well enough with his mature viewpoint. For in requiring a unifying vision from the modern poet, Read had assigned him the role of truth-bringer and law-giver.

IV

CREATIVE EXPRESSION AND POETIC TRADITION

1

By the late 1920's, Read had managed to 'sanction' poetry by identifying it with an intuitive mode of cognition which furnishes a direct and immediate knowledge of an ultimate 'pattern' or unity. Since this mode "involves everything", poetry was safe: it could not be reduced through the discursive, analytical process of 'science'. Yet some very difficult questions remained. Poetry is this intuitive mode, Read had said, "under the aspect of expression", but he had left expression as much a mystery in 1928 as in 1918. His theory accounted for essence but not for its embodiment; it accounted for 'poetry' but not for a poem.

His difficulties had been apparent in his essay on metaphysical poetry, where he had ended by projecting a contemporary poetry of mathematical physics. Yet what such a poetry would be like is hard to imagine. The kind of aesthetic realization of mathematical abstractions Read had in mind seems far more appropriate to a visual medium, with its purely formal possibilities, than to poetry: and it is significant that in recent years he was looking not to poetry for this realization but to the 'constructivism' of the sculptor, Naum Gabo.[1] It was to a vision of pure plastic form that his argument in this essay finally led him. Now while the difficulties he faced in regard to a contemporary metaphysical poetry were particularly acute, they were not essentially different from the difficulties involved in lyrical poetry. Whether the object of the poet's vision was an abstraction or a part of the phenomenal environment made no difference to the process of poetry. For the effect of Read's distinction between modes of cognition had been to throw expression into two distinct kinds: the temporal process

---

[1] See "Constructivism; The Art of Naum Gabo and Antoine Pevsner" *The Philosophy of Modern Art* (New York, 1953).

of discourse, and the non-temporal, instantaneous act of poetry. Thus in both metaphysical and lyrical poetry, an intuitive apprehension must issue as an act of expression altogether different from the process of discourse.

It was to the implications of his 'sanction' for poetry that Read addressed himself in the late 1920's and early 1930's and particularly to the consequences that followed from dividing expression into two distinct kinds. These consequences led him increasingly to attempt to establish an unconscious and instinctual basis for poetry. He had already been probing in this direction for some time, looking particularly for evidence from psychology and physiology. In his essay on metaphysical poetry, for example, he had conjectured that there might be a physiological basis for the distinction between lyrical and metaphysical poetry – a distinction that depended on the existence of 'concrete' and 'abstract' emotions. "Physiology may yet identify and classify the various glandular excretions and their appropriate lyrical responses", he said. "Nor am I disposed to deny that the state of attention or contemplation induced by metaphysical poetry may not also have its basis in some material agitation of the human cortex or glandular system."[2] The more firmly Read could establish poetry as an activity deeply rooted in the human constitution, the more convincing his entire argument would be, and he grasped eagerly at any scientific evidence that seemed promising. So it was that the new doctrines of psychoanalysis proved to a powerful attraction for him. In the *Criterion* in 1925 he published an essay, "Psycho-analysis and the Critic" (reprinted in *Reason and Romanticism* as "Psychoanalysis and Criticism"), in which he surveyed the theories of Freud, Jung, and Adler, taking from them whatever seemed to be useful. "As a mere expropriator in this territory I take the liberty to lift my material from whichever quarter suits me best".[3] he said. Approaching these doctrines in this cavalier fashion, he believed he had found considerable support for his view of poetry and the poetic process. For example, Jung's notion of 'phantasy' as a perpetually creative act which unites subject and object, thought and feeling, idea and

---

[2] "The Nature of Metaphysical Poetry", *Reason and Romanticism*, p. 33.

[3] "Psychoanalysis and Criticism", *Reason and Romanticism*, p. 89. First published in the *Criterion*, III, 10 (1925), 214—230, and later reprinted, with considerable revisions and additions, in *Collected Essays in Literary Criticism* under the title, "The Nature of Criticism".

thing, indicated to him that poetry has its basis in a very fundamental psychic activity. Read, however, wanted to push this notion farther than Jung had gone with it.

Although Jung remarks that this active phantasy is "the principal attribute of the artistic mentality" he nowhere seems to have pressed home the conclusions which are surely latent in his theory, namely, that the poetic function is nothing else but this active phantasy in its more-than-individual aspect. The poet, in fact, is one who is capable of creating phantasies of more than individual use – phantasies, as we should say, of universal appeal. Thus art has for psychoanalysis the general function of resolving into one uniform flow of life all that springs from the inner well of primordial images and instinctive feelings, and all that springs from the outer mechanism of actuality – doing this, not only for the artist himself, from whose own need the phantasy is born, but also, by suggestion and by symbol, for all who come to participate in his imaginative work.[4]

To give poetry this kind of universal integrative function is to assign it a role like that of myth or religion. And thus it is not surprising to find that Read was particularly impressed with Jung's notion of a collective unconscious, and that he was interested in the possibility of "relating the types actualised by the poetic imagination to their origin in the root-images of the community". For this meant that poetry had its basis in the "collective ideas or primordial images" which "crystallize" as myths and religions. Read even suggested that, since the symbols of religion have become ineffective in the modern world, the psychologist might "unite with the critic" to "indicate the needs of the collective mind".[5] In this way he proposed perhaps as grand a mission for the contemporary critic as he had for the contemporary metaphysical poet.

For his view of the poetic process as a creative moment, or series of such moments, Read believed he had found confirmation in psychoanalytical doctrines. He maintained in this essay that the poet's mind is characterized by two contrary tendencies: in one direction he slips into the "disjointed fortuitous world of dreams – day dreams", the "rich though incoherent fantasy" of his "primitive mind"; in the other he establishes "strong affective tendencies – ideals of moral beauty, of plastic form, of order and architecture".[6]

[4] *Ibid.*, pp. 90—91.
[5] *Ibid.*, p. 106.
[6] *Ibid.*, p. 92.

Such ideals, Read thought, could be explained by means of Adler's notion of the inferiority complex. The "buried sense of superiority is present in most of us", Read said, "but the artist takes the goal of godlikeness seriously and is compelled to flee from real life and compromise to seek a life within life; and he is an artist by virtue of the form and ideal perfection which he can give to this inner life."[7] The creative process, then, arises from an interaction between these two opposed tendencies. Read described it in this way:

You have in the first place the prevailing affectivity, the latent ideal of form or thought ... You have, next, the bringing into activity fortuitously of some image or memory which until the moment of inspiration had lain latent in the unconscious mind; this fortuitous image is as it were criticized by the excited interest; it is selected or rejected; and if selected it is developed and transformed by the ever prevalent affectivity. If the affective tendency is suddenly and strongly roused, then you get a state of emotion, bringing with it an intensity of awareness to all the images and ideas that follow in the wake of the first fortuitous image. This is the state of ecstasy. Images seem to leap from their hiding-places all fully equipped for the service of the ideal or affective tendency. But even in this state of animation or ecstasy I believe that a good deal of selection and rejection of images still goes on. However, normally a creative act occurs when the exact word or image is found. And the full creative process is but a summation of many of these primary creative moments.[8]

A comparison of this version of the creative process with the one Read had set forth in 1918[9] shows that, although the terms are different and the detail furnished is greater, nothing essential has been changed. The process is still confined to a moment, or a series of moments, and it still consists in the sudden discovery of the 'exact' word or image. The place of 'intellect', or 'intelligence', in the earlier version is now taken by the "affective tendencies" (a more accurate term, since the activity in question is really emotional, springing from a desire for ideal beauty, ideal form, or as he had previously called it, the 'aesthetic absolute'). Where he had earlier pictured 'intellect' as selecting and rejecting 'emotions' according to their 'aesthetic worth', he now said the 'excited interest' performs this function among the 'fortuitous' images, ideas, or memories which rise from the unconscious mind. In neither version is there

[7] *Ibid.*, p. 97.
[8] *Ibid.*, pp. 94—95.
[9] See above, pp. 22—26.

any place for intellectual activity in the sense of deliberate construction and shaping, and thus in neither is there any place for technique. The only technique Read mentioned in "Psychoanalysis and Criticism" was a 'technique of inspiration'. He said that "the part that may be played by suggestion or self-hypnosis in the encouragement of such states is obviously considerable, and I think that in time a complete technique of inspiration may be evolved".[10] Thus the creative process was for Read something over which the poet had little control; the most he could hope for was to learn how to induce the creative state.

Whether very much of this description of the poetic process actually came from Read's psychoanalytical sources is, I think, doubtful. He claimed that it "is based both on my reading of psychology and on the analysis of my own putative experiences";[11] but one cannot help feeling that there is more of the latter than of the former in it. It seems to be in the main an account of the way Read wrote poetry, or believed he wrote it. What is important in this essay is not the somewhat fanciful character of this supposedly 'scientific' description of the creative process, nor, as Häusermann has pointed out, the naïveté with which ideas are combined from a number of different psychoanalytical sources.[12] What is important is Read's insistence on finding a way to account for poetry wholly outside the rational intellect. And one must remember that he wrote this essay while aligned with the classicists, intellectualists, and anti-romanticists of post-war criticism. Behind his 'intellectualism' lay an extreme form of the romantic doctrine of inspiration, for which he believed he had found scientific confirmation in psychoanalytical theory.

In another essay published in 1925, "The Future of Poetry",[13] Read maintained that science had proven the case for the unconscious

[10] "Psychoanalysis and Criticism", loc. cit., p. 95.

[11] Ibid.

[12] "The contradictions in Read's theory of the poetic imagination are numerous; they are easily discovered even by a person untrained in psychology ... The invoked authorities with their different presuppositions are used without distinction in support of Read's theory, without their field of application having been duly defined ...". — H. W. Häusermann, "The Development of Herbert Read", loc. cit., p. 66.

[13] Times Literary Supplement, Sep. 10, 1925, 573—574; reprinted in Reason and Romanticism, and (in part) in Collected Essays in Literary Criticism.

or instinctual nature of poetic rhythm. He contended that experimental research with the kymograph had shown quantity to be a "structural element in . . . English verse, side by side with accent", indicating that poetic rhythm was a matter of "ratios of duration". The consequence of this discovery, he held, was a substitution of "the element of proportion in rhythm for the element of regularity; and this is precisely what the best *vers libriste* poets, in France, England, and America, have been contending for".[14] Now Read had maintained from the beginning that the poet's rhythm was determined by his emotion; yet rhythm presented a difficult problem for him because it is a temporal phenomenon, while his conception of poetic form was so exclusively oriented toward the image as to be virtually spatial. Thus in 1918 he had listed rhythm among the various 'decorations' which the poet might use, the implication being that the poet applied them consciously and deliberately. The effect of his argument in "The Future of Poetry", however, was to make rhythm a constitutive, not a decorative, element in poetic form. He took the evidence from kymograph research to mean that poetic rhythm could now be accounted for as a wholly instinctual phenomenon. No rhythms – not even in traditional verse, he said, can be regarded as "variations on the basis of a regular measure". None are "consciously constructed by a system of normal measurements: they are rather spontaneous sense perceptions". Their basis is in 'idioms', which are the "live organism of speech".

Now this organic unit, this idiom, is instinct with rhythm; it has irrefrangible intonation, and poetic rhythm is but the extension and the aggregation of these primary rhythms. Even measured, regularly accented verse is successful only in so far as it makes use of or accommodates itself to these idioms. Free verse, which includes the slightest as well as the widest divergence from regular pattern, is but the free use of these idioms.[15]

Read's aim here was to explain poetic rhythm wholly on the basis of its instinctual origin. For him to conceive it as being constructed on the basis of a regular measure would have been to admit a rational principle into its formation. This he could not do. He could not even conceive it as lying somewhere between the

---

[14] "The Future of Poetry", *Reason and Romanticism*, p. 76.
[15] *Ibid.*, p. 79.

strictness of a regular measure and the license of spontaneous sense perceptions. He was determined, rather, to account for the regularity of the measure on the basis of the spontaneity of the sense perceptions. In this way every kind of poetic rhythm, even the most traditional, became actually spontaneous and instinctual, although 'free verse' represented of course the most direct and honest realization of this spontaneity. Having in this way removed any taint of rationality in the formation of poetic rhythm, he could regard it as a constitutive element in poetic form. Even so, he had not – as became evident later – overcome the difficulty of its inherent temporality.

2

These first probings into the psycho-physical basis of poetry prepared the way for a radical view of poetic expression and poetic tradition. In 1928 Read published *English Prose Style*. This book was actually an 'art' of prose – an analysis of the means and techniques used in composition and rhetoric – and, while we are not concerned here with Read's study of this art, the distinctions he made between prose expression and poetic expression are very important. An 'art' of poetry was for Read quite impossible: 'art', in the sense of a deliberate exercise of technique, belonged only to what he called 'constructive' expression. 'Poetry', he said in the preface to *English Prose Style*, "is the expression of one form of mental activity, Prose is the expression of another form. Poetry is creative expression; Prose is constructive expression."[16] Thus the distinction between them was one of kind, not of degree. Moreover, it corresponded exactly with his distinction between modes of cognition: on the one hand an instantaneous act; on the other, a process in time. "By 'creative' I mean *original*", he said. "In Poetry the words are born or re-born in the act of thinking. The words are, in Bergsonian phraseology, a becoming; they develop in the mind *pari passu* with the development of the thought. The thought is the word and the word is thought, and both the thought and the word are Poetry."[17] The consequence was that

[16] *English Prose Style* (London, 1928), p. x. The second edition (New York, 1952) is much revised, but the distinctions I discuss here remain unaltered.
[17] *Ibid.*, p. x.

poetry, according to Read, "may inhere in a single word, in a single syllable", and may thus paradoxically be "without rhythm". Prose, on the other hand, "does not exist except in the phrase, and the phrase always has rhythm of some kind".[18] Here, then, was Read's admission that, in the final analysis, rhythm in poetry is ancillary. Having made a TEMPORAL distinction between two modes of cognition and two modes of expression, he had no way of including rhythm – despite its unconscious or instinctual basis – in the essential creative act.

"'Constructive'", Read said, "implies ready-made materials; words stacked round the builder, ready for use. Prose is a structure of ready-made words. Its 'creative' function is confined to plan and elevation– functions these, too, of Poetry, but in Poetry subsidiary to the creative function."[19] Thus Read did not necessarily rule rational construction out of poetry, but its function had to be at any rate clearly subsidiary. The "poetic" element in poetry remained always the 'original' word born in the creative act, and in this act construction had no place. Behind this view of poetry as an 'act of thinking' in which "the thought is the word and the word is thought", lay the notion that the poet's mentality is more primitive than the prose writer's, representing a pre-logical and pre-conceptual stage of human development. This notion, which goes back to Vico, Read was to make more use of later, when it merged in his thinking with similar ideas from psychoanalysis. For his distinction between two kinds of expression, however, it meant that the poet's use of language is altogether different from the prose writer's: synthetic rather than analytical, metaphorical rather than conceptual. Thus in *English Prose Style*, although he considered metaphor as a technical device of the prose writer, he ended by assigning it mainly to poetry:

Metaphor . . . is the synthesis of several units of observation into one commanding image; it is the expression of a complex idea, not by analysis, nor by abstract statement, but by a sudden perception of an objective relation. The complex idea is translated into a concrete equivalent.[20]

---

[18] *Ibid.*, p. xi.
[19] *Ibid.*, p. xi.
[20] *Ibid.*, p. 25.

Whatever we may say of [metaphor], and however great and inclusive the function we assign to it, essentially it belongs to the sphere of poetry. Poetry alone is creative. The art of prose is not creative, but constructive or logical.[21]

The term 'imagination' Read also reserved chiefly for poetry. 'Imagination', he said, ". . . is 'the creative faculty of the mind.' It is creative, if we keep to the etymological significance of the word, in that it bodies forth 'images.' In this sense I maintain that it is a poetical faculty. The 'maker' of imagery is the poet." For prose Read assigned the term 'invention' rather than 'imagination'.[22] It is significant that he should have tried here to confine the term 'imagination' to the bodying forth of images, for such was in fact the poetic process in its entirety, as he conceived it: an instantaneous act in which an equivalence is reached between thought and word – or, as he variously described it, between emotion and image, or idea and image.

Read's distinction between two kinds of mental activity, 'creative' and 'constructive', cut across all formal distinctions between poetry and prose. We might, that is, find 'poetry' in prose, or 'prose' in poetry. As to how to recognize 'poetry', however, he was not very helpful. "I frankly resort to a personal doctrine", he said. "Observation convinces me that in poetry, as in every other art, the people who recognize the art are few, and that these few recognize it instinctively . . . . The difference between poetry and prose is a qualitative difference that has its effects in expression, but . . . these effects cannot be measured quantitatively, but only by the exercise of an instinctive judgment."[23] Thus his doctrine of a temporal difference between poetic and rational expression inevitably made of the former something which could only be recognized in the same way it was attained – instinctively, intuitively, immediately.

So it was that when Read looked at the tradition of English poetry he exercised his 'instinctive judgment'. In the same year *English Prose Style* appeared (1928), he published *Phases of English Poetry*, a small volume in which he attempted to select a tradition for modern poetry. In the preface he stated that he looked at the past with the eye of the modern poet, not the historical student:

[21] *Ibid.*, p. 34.
[22] *Ibid.*, pp. 156—157.
[23] *Ibid.*, pp. xi—xii.

"For the existing state of affairs (or the existing state of consciousness) certain authors have no immediacy, no impelling influence, no sympathetic power .... I have treated as poets only those whose poetry has for me the air of present reality."[24] This is to say that he was seeking a viable tradition, a usable past, for modern poetry. Other post-war critics, most notably Eliot and Pound, had been engaged in the same search, and each had found somewhat different traditions. Read's, however, turned out to be of an altogether different order. He selected from the past not so much what was useful to the modern poet as what was absolutely poetry, in this way dividing tradition radically into poetry and non-poetry.

Read chose those poets whose sensibilities appeared to him to be genuine. His view of tradition was based on his conviction that poetry is an essence which corresponds to something in the poet's nature – his sensibility, he called it here – and that the poetic essence has taken a variety of forms according to the age in which the poet lived:

Poetic sensibility – it is one of the axioms of this book – does not determine poetic form. It only yields the poetic essence – the quality without which there is no poetry, but which alone would be a disembodied quality, hard to imagine. Actually the essence surrenders to material associations; it becomes linked with the diction and thought of the poet. These in their turn owe almost everything to the spirit of the age; the poet depends on his social and cultural environment – not for his poetic sensibility, which is innate, but for opportunity and occasion to manifest this sensibility.[25]

Read traced the manifestation of poetic sensibility through five 'phases': the anonymous and communal ballads; the humanistic poetry of the Renaissance; the metaphysical poetry of the seventeenth century; the poetry of the romantic revival; and contemporary post-war 'modern' poetry. The principal poets he discussed were Chaucer, Spenser, Donne, Crashaw, and Wordsworth; their sensibilities, manifesting themselves in accordance with the 'spirit of the age' had formed a tradition which had for Read 'the air of present reality'. The work of Milton, Dryden, and Pope, on the other hand, was 'without significance':

[24] *Phases of English Poetry* (London, 1928), p. 5.
[25] *Ibid.*, p. 47.

To compare [Milton's] diction with Crashaw's (or with Donne's) is to realise that what he took he polished, and that the lustre which he gave to English verse, though brilliant, is not vital ... If polish were a phase (instead of an aspect or reflection) there would be more to say of Milton's poetry, and of the general development of English poetry during the second half of the seventeenth and first half of the eighteenth centuries. But great as is my admiration for the poetic diction of Dryden and Pope, and for the critical understanding upon which that diction is based, I cannot help concluding that it is without significance for the present inquiry. It was essentially a period of refining (as of refinement); they refined on Chaucer and on Spenser, on Shakespeare and on Donne but they made no movement.[26]

Polish and refinement are of course matters of 'art', and so the work of Milton, Dryden, and Pope could not be considered a 'phase' of poetic consciousness. Indeed, Read did not consider Pope to be a poet at all. "Pope's virtues, which are very great, belong to a sphere which is scarcely poetical in the limited meaning given to poetry for the purpose of these lectures. They belong to the sphere which Dryden called 'wit-writing,' and in that sphere they are unrivaled."[27] Read was beginning here to distinguish his second, or 'false', tradition – a tradition of 'art', or 'wit-writing', which belonged to 'constructive' rather than 'creative' expression, and about which he was to have more to say later.

Although Read used the term 'development' throughout *Phases of English Poetry*, its application to his view of tradition was somewhat complicated. In sensibility, for example, there was no development at all. He remarked that Spenser's "poetic idiom is still the best standard or touchstone of English poetic sensibility ... Spenser's form is the form of his age; his sensibility is inherent in our language; the present need should be a modern form embodying Spenser's sensibility".[28] And in the notion of a poetic essence, there is of course an assumption of something permanent and unchanging, for which the whole concept of historical development is quite irrelevant: "In a sense, Shakespeare *is* English poetry. He represents its essence. ..."[29] What does change, then, is the manner of expression, and this is determined by "the spirit of the age". Yet even here there was a distinction, in Read's view,

[26] *Ibid.*, pp. 81–82.
[27] *Ibid.*, pp. 87–88.
[28] *Ibid.*, p. 45.
[29] *Ibid.*, p. 6.

between the poet's diction and his thoughts and beliefs. In keeping with his conception of an equivalence between poetic thought and poetic word, of a simultaneity of apprehension and expression, Read maintained that the poet's sensibility is registered directly in his diction. Poetic diction is thus a kind of permanent indication of poetic sensibility, even though vocabularies may change. And thoughts and beliefs, which are subject to historical development, have no necessary connection with diction:

The relation of poetic diction to poetic thought is a comparatively unexplored subject; I am not sure that there is any necessary connection between them at all. His diction makes or mars the poet; it is the expression of his sensibility, and as such is unequivocal. The thought of the poet is a factor which will enhance his general "value", but it does not alter his poetic value.[30]
Beliefs or sentiments of any kind never constitute poetry; they only modify it. Poetry is primarily a matter of words ... and any particular phase ... is mainly the effect of the use of a particular vocabulary.[31]

Thus to trace the poetic essence is to trace poetic sensibility as registered in diction and modified by the thoughts and beliefs, techniques and forms of the age.

The only development which Read's tradition could be said to have undergone was a historical progress from objectivity to subjectivity. "Poetry has developed from the widest possible appeal – an appeal commensurate with the community itself – to the narrowest possible appeal – the poet appealing to himself alone. A circle has been completed – completed only within the last generation or two."[32] The central chapters of *Phases of English Poetry* are concerned with the change from the relative objectivity of Spenser, who "kept to the visual significance of words", to the subjectivity of Crashaw and Wordsworth, who each had a "personal idiom" of a "peculiar intensity".[33] This idiom was the consequence of their 'mystical' or 'ecstatic' state of being, which Read indentified with the poetic state itself:

Crashaw's mystical state of being, when sense and discourse are suspended to let in faith for the sake of the skill and the force which faith can give – this state is also the poetic state. In the act of writing his

[30] *Ibid.*, p. 50.
[31] *Ibid.*, p. 57.
[32] *Ibid.*, p. 10.
[33] *Ibid.*, p. 102.

poem the poet enters on a state in which feeling and reasoning are for the moment suspended, and only intuition is operative.[34]
Wordsworth attained towards Nature the same kind of mystical faith that Crashaw attained towards his God, and this faith was an ecstatic state of being which can be identified with the poetic state. It is the mood induced by worship, but by worship intense beyond the conception of normal minds.[35]

Read meant that Crashaw's and Wordsworth's mystical apprehensions of God and Nature were profound intuitions of unity, and as such were poetic states. "Crashaw's transcendent God, Wordsworth's immanent spirit of the Universe", he said, "are perhaps the noblest religious ideals ever formulated in the history of English thought; and yet they are but aspects of poetic experience."[36]

The mysticism of Crashaw and Wordsworth, however, was for Read only a stage in the refinement of poetic apprehension, leading to the relatively pure state represented by modern poetry. In modern poetry, he said, all doctrines have been abandoned except the doctrine of sincerity.

Wordsworth's sincerity effected a revolution in English poetic diction. Modern poetry has carried that revolution a step further.[37]
The modern poet has no uncompromising theory of metrical composition. His theory, if any, is that it is sufficient to be a poet and to be honest with one's self, and that the rest follows naturally ... He ... affirms that poetry is sincerity, and has no essential alliance with regular schemes of any sort. He reserves the right to adapt his rhythm to his mood, to modulate his metre as he progresses.[38]

The result, Read said, was not a "simple and artless" poetry, but one often complicated and obscure.

By definition a poet is a being of abnormal sensibility, and the reactions of such a being to the complex problems of existence ... are sure to be of a complexity quite beyond the normal limits of expression. Where he cannot see clearly, the poet will be driven to divine intuitively, and to express himself analogically, by means of metaphor, symbol, and allegory. It would be possible to say, were the word not so debased, that he resorted to mysticism.[39]

[34] *Ibid.*, p. 78.
[35] *Ibid.*, p. 102.
[36] *Ibid.*, p. 106.
[37] *Ibid.*, p. 144.
[38] *Ibid.*, p. 146.
[39] *Ibid.*, p. 151.

Yet to achieve successful expression in modern poetry, Read believed, requires even more discipline than in traditional poetry. "Far from seeking freedom and irresponsibility ... [the modern poet] seeks a stricter discipline, which is the exact concord to thought and feeling, the discipline of sincerity."[40] And the genuineness of his poetry can be tested only by its sincerity. "You must test the modern poet as you would test your friends: by faith and familiarity and a perfect knowledge."[41] Finally, Read acknowledged that the modern poet should, ideally, "enter again into the first phase of the historical development of poetry, and become the insidious inspirer of a fresh communal poetry",[42] but that he himself preferred to continue the research into subjectivity.

Inwardly I feel that this life of the intelligence is the only reality, and that the art of poetry is the difficult art of defining the nature of mind and emotion – a veiled activity, leading the poet deep into the obscurities of the human heart.[43]

For an 'absolute' poetry, then, Read sought an 'absolute' tradition. He saw tradition as the manifestation of poetic sensibility in several historic 'phases', no one of which can be said to be 'better' than another. From the standpoint of the sensibility manifested there has been no development. But from the standpoint of the directness and honesty with which the poet expresses his sensibility, one can trace a progressive refinement culminating in modern poetry. There has been, in other words, a historical progress toward the isolation of poetic apprehension in its purity: an advance toward a mystical state, the genuineness of which can only be tested by the sincerity of the poet. When we try to discover how this state is registered in poetry, however, we are confronted with the same dilemma we have noted before: there is no way to get from essence to embodiment. The poet's sensibility is registered directly in his diction, Read said, and apparently that was for him the end of the matter, either a genuine sensibility has expressed itself in the genuine diction of poetry or it has not.

---

40 *Ibid.*, pp. 153–154.
41 *Ibid.*, p. 154.
42 *Ibid.*, p. 155.
43 *Ibid.*, p. 158.

3

To account for poetic expression had from the beginning been more difficult for Read than to account for poetic vision, and as we watch him wrestling with the problem in *Phases of English Poetry* we can see that he was still far from a solution. Indeed, he was hardly any nearer being able to account for a poem than he had been in 1918. What he needed was a principle of poetic form that would not be dependent in any way on the rational mind, and such a principle he had not yet formulated, although his studies of psychoanalysis had shown it to be feasible. Thus his struggles in *Phases of English Poetry* with the problem of expression were bound to be inconclusive. Nevertheless, we can gain from them a clearer idea of the nature of poetic expression than ever before, and particularly we can come closer to knowing what he meant by 'exact' expression.

Above all else, Read said, poetry was not to be "an emotional evocation of an emotional state",[44] and on this basis he sought to dissociate himself from the French critic, the Abbé Brémond, and his doctrine of *la poésie pure*. Although Read himself held a theory of absolute poetry, he was reluctant to use the term 'pure' because of its association with this French school. Despite his own identification of the poetic state with the mystical state, he objected to Brémond's identification of poetry and prayer. Prayer was for Read quite the opposite of creation. He said that Brémond "ignores the distinction between an objective and a subjective activity, between a godlike and rebellious creativity in man, and man's most utter renunciation of selfhood".[45] It must be kept in mind that the term 'mysticism', as used by Read in relation to poetry, meant always a mysticism "under the aspect of expression". The poetic state is a moment in which apprehension and expression exist in a complex – thought becomes word, subjective becomes objective. The Abbé's identification of poetry and prayer, however, and his emphasis on the incantatory magic of poetry, meant for Read a 'rendering' of the flow of emotion and an avoidance of the difficulty involved in the poetic state – the difficulty of 'exact expression', of the 'discipline of sincerity':

[44] *Ibid.*, p. 122.
[45] *Ibid.*, p. 124, n. 1.

Emotion is not rendered by emotion; there are events, emotions, states of soul (call them what you will) on the one side, and on the other side are certain symbols, namely, words, which in themselves are objective facts, and the process of expression, poetic or otherwise, is nothing but the translation of the one category into terms of the other. ...

This is no less than the problem of art or no art – of whether the writer is to control his means of expression (keep his eye on the object, as we say), or whether he is merely to abandon himself to the stream of feeling – to incantations, evocations, vague reveries, and false mysticism. In one case arduous effort, continuous self-criticism, and a definite ideal; in the other case, at the best, an inspired delirium, at the worst, the actual decomposition of intelligence.[46]

Here again is Read's insistence that emotion be objectified: that the 'stream of feeling' be arrested and fixed in an image, rather than rendered in its flow. The magic of poetry lay for him in the process by which this is done, not in incantations. For the "romantic phraseology of the Brémond type" he said he would substitute the single term 'Imagination' – "all the magic and mystery of poetry is summarised in this one word imagination". The elements of poetry, he held, can be reduced to three: sound, sense, and suggestion. They all "admit of objective analysis; they can be explained without any resort to mystery or magic. But the power of combining them – the power, that is to say, of relating words to thoughts – this is the power of imagination."[47] Thus for Read the mystery of poetry lay not in the elements which composed it – these were objective enough – but in the process by which an equivalence was reached between them and the poet's 'thought'.

Although this process remains a mystery in *Phases of English Poetry* (and indeed Read has never really managed to explain it), we can, by putting together some scattered remarks in this book, arrive at a better understanding of the two sides of the equation. On the objective or verbal side, the "equivalence" could consist in simply a visual image, non-metaphorical and non-musical. Of some lines he quoted, for example, he said that they were "simple statements devoid of metaphor or extraordinary musical delight . . the poetical effect is one of visual imagery . . . the words are merely means to the visual images; the poetry resides not in musical delight, but in visual delight – not the direct visual delight of

[46] *Ibid.*, pp. 122 – 123.
[47] *Ibid.*, pp. 127 – 128.

plastic art, but the joy of the 'inward eye' ".[48] To achieve an equivalence for the greatest visions, however, metaphor was apparently
necessary. Shakespeare, for example, whose 'most distinguishing
quality' was metaphor, represented for Read the 'essence' of English
poetry. To the 'grace and fluidity' of Spenser, Read said, Shakespeare had added a "wealth of metaphors".

Spenser, in spite of his continual use of allegory, kept to the visual significance of words; each word distinct and separate, pebbles in the stream.
But now words were to flash with interverbal meaning; they no longer
reflect an equivalent and logical meaning; the become mere sounds
and symbols suggesting a meaning beyond the compass of words, clear
only to the intuitive vision of the poet. Words dissolve and lose their
outlines in such a fierce glory.[49]

On the verbal side of the equation, then, metaphor is supreme,
and in its higher reaches it apparently becomes for Read not
a device of art but an instrument of apprehension.

This is what we should expect, of course, from his division of
expression into synthetic or metaphorical, and analytic or discursive,
modes. Yet the surprising thing is that for his future development
the metaphorical equivalence is of less importance than the simple
visual equivalence. For we shall find him in the 1930's, when the
implications of psychoanalysis have been more fully worked out,
rejecting metaphor in favor of a doctrine of the image which equates
it with the dream and makes of it something wholly visual.

On the other side of the equation – where lie those "events,
emotions, states of soul (call them what you will)" – we can find in
Phases of English Poetry a certain amount of clarification about the
'event' which Read called 'thought'. Throughout the book he used
the words 'thought' and 'emotion' almost interchangeably, for in
his view thought in poetry IS emotion and yet remains thought. "In
poetry the thought is emotional (I use the phrase in full consciousness of its paradoxicality)", he said. He perhaps came closest to
explaining the nature of this paradox in the course of his discussion
of sincerity in modern poetry. Under the doctrine of sincerity,
he said, the poet

describes as he sees, and he thinks as he feels (this is not to say, however,
that he thinks *when* he feels; that would be to subordinate thought to

[48] *Ibid.*, p. 127.
[49] *Ibid.*, p. 56.

feeling. I mean that thought, which has its own logical processes, pursues a path which always runs parallel to the process of feeling. Thought can at any moment be tested by reference to its accompanying state of sensibility. And, *vice versa*, a state of sensibility can always be tested by reference to its accompanying process of thought. Sensibility unaccompanied by thought is sentimentality).[50]

Read meant, I believe, that thought, if not based in emotion, is mere discursive ratiocination, the cold analytical process of 'science'. And emotion, without thought against which to test it, is mere sentimentality. Neither, alone, is poetic. Yet Read had allowed himself no way of bringing them together in the creative moment except by making thought a species of intuition – nondiscursive and nontemporal. Indeed, he had no way even of discussing the process without resorting to the same kind of poetic metaphors he was trying to explain. Thus he said, in relation to Crashaw's metaphysical poetry, that "when passion . . . is directed to ideas and essences, all the intangible universals of thought and meditation . . . the poet resorts to emotional analogies – to words which give, not *meaning* which cannot be given, but an equivalence of tone, of colour, an equivalence of the *pattern* and contour of thought".[51] The phrase "contour of thought" Read has used a number of times since, without ever attempting to explain it. The fact is, it cannot be explained. To Read, thought becomes in poetry an entity which can only be described in visual terms. Discourse gives the meaning, poetry the contour, of thought. Thought, emotion, and feeling merge in a poetic cognition which is also an act of expression.

The argument of *Phases of English Poetry* is sometimes hard to accept; yet it is consistent, and it follows directly from Read's division of expression into two distinct kinds – 'creative' and 'constructive'. Once this division is made, each kind must then be considered separately. The tradition of English prose can be studied as the development of an art; the tradition of English poetry, however, must be approached as an inexplicable and unpredictable manifestation of an absolute essence.

[50] *Ibid.*, p. 144.
[51] *Ibid.*, p. 74.

V

PERSONALITY AND POETIC FORM

1

The year 1932 marks a watershed in Read's development, for with the publication of *Form in Modern Poetry* in that year he began to emerge as a theorist of modern poetry working consciously and avowedly in the tradition of Coleridge. Before 1932, we hardly know what to call his position; after 1932, we can describe it as romantic, in the sense that he derived the principle of organic form from Coleridge and sought to establish modern poetry as a continuation, or completion, of the romantic movement of the early nineteenth century. *Form in Modern Poetry* is thus a key book in his development, as well as a contribution of some significance to the theory of modern poetry, and its argument deserves a fairly detailed examination.

As we look back on Read's development, we can see that *Form in Modern Poetry* does not represent a sudden reversal of field. Rather, it is a continuation of the argument begun in the late 1920's which we have considered in the last chapter. Having made a distinction in kind between poetic and prose expression, and having selected an absolute poetic tradition, he needed a theoretical principle which would do two things: account for the FORM of poetic expression as opposed to prose expression, and furnish a basis for his absolute tradition by accounting for the fact that some poets produce genuine poetry and some do not. Read's division of expression into two kinds made it necessary for him to show that the poem is 'formed' in the expressive act, *i.e.*, before any conscious, deliberate construction or shaping can take place. To do this he had to advance a very radical notion of poetic 'personality' as the basis for organic form. Thus where Eliot had offered an 'impersonal' theory for modern poetry, Read proposed an extremely 'personal' one:

This is where I take my stand, even against my best friends in criticism, such as Mr. Eliot himself. I believe that criticism must concern itself, not only with the work of art in itself, but also with the process of writing, and the writer's state of mind when inspired – that is to say, criticism must concern itself, not only with the finished work of art, but also with the workman, his mental activity and his tools. If that is not admitted, no really useful progress can be made in this essay.[1]

Read began with a distinction between 'organic' and 'abstract' form which appeared virtually identical with Coleridge's distinction between 'organic' and 'mechanic' form. Coleridge had said:

The form is mechanic when on any given material we impress a predetermined form, not necessarily arising out of the properties of the material ... The organic form, on the other hand, is innate; it shapes, as it develops, itself from within, and the fulness of its development is one and the same with the perfection of its outward form.[2]

Read defined 'organic' and 'abstract' form in this way:

When a work of art has its own inherent laws, originating with its very invention and fusing in one vital unity both structure and content, then the resulting form may be described as *organic*.

When an organic form is stabilised and repeated as a pattern, and the intention of the artist is no longer related to the inherent dynamism of an inventive act, but seeks to adapt content to predetermined structure, then the resulting form may be described as *abstract*.[3]

Although Read's distinction sounds like Coleridge's, it is actually much more radical. Coleridge had required the exercise of the conscious will in poetry. His idea of an innate principle of form brought ALL the mind into play in the creation of a work of art. Read, however, could not do this. His real distinction was between two modes of apprehension, and the only way he could keep the expression of these modes separate was to give each its own principle of form. To find the principle for 'constructive' expression he could turn to the rational intellect, as he had done in *English Prose Style*. To find it for 'creative' expression he had to look toward a deeper, less conscious level of the mind: he had to be able to

[1] *Form in Modern Poetry* (New York, 1933), p. 8. Published in England in 1932.

[2] S. T. Coleridge, *Shakespearean Criticism*, ed. T. M. Raysor (London, 1960), Vol. I, p. 198.

[3] *Form in Modern Poetry*, pp. 3–4.

account for form in 'creative' expression without involving 'constructive' expression in the creative process. It was for this reason that he advanced his notion of 'personality'. "Before we can see how organic form takes shape", he said, "we must first consider the nature of the poet's personality; for upon the nature of his personality depends the form of his poetry".[4]

On exactly the same lines that he had distinguished two kinds of cognition and two kinds of expression, Read now proceeded to distinguish two kinds of psychological structures: the 'character' and the 'personality'.

Character ... is an impersonal ideal which the individual selects and to which he sacrifices all other claims, especially those of the sentiments or emotions. It follows that character must be placed in opposition to personality, which is the general-common-denominator of our sentiments and emotions. That is, indeed, the opposition I wish to emphasise; and when I have said further that all poetry, in which I include all lyrical impulses whatsoever, is the product of the personality, and therefore inhibited in a character, I have stated the main theme of my essay.[5]

Read tried to relate these concepts to Freud's division of the mind into conscious, preconscious, and unconscious levels, but the relationship is not altogether clear. The real difference between character and personality lies in the manner in which the ego is organized, an idea which he apparently did not get from Freud. Freud had pictured the ego as mediator between the id and external reality, the agent that brings the pleasure-principle into conformity with the reality principle. What concerned Read, however, was not the ego's mediatory function but its organization. Freud, he said, had defined the ego as 'a coherent organisation of mental processes'. Read was interested in the nature of this organization: is it imposed from without, or does it proceed from within? The difference between these two kinds of coherence, he thought, is the difference between 'character' and 'personality'.

The coherence of character, Read said, is based on repression and inhibition:

Character can be explained as a disposition in the individual due to the repression of certain impulses which would otherwise be present in the personality; it is therefore something more restricted than personality.

[4] *Ibid.*, p. 5.
[5] *Ibid.*, pp. 18—19.

Character, which always has such a positive aspect, is really the result of certain fixities or negations imposed on the flow of consciousness. A flood only gains character and direction when it is confined between banks.[6]

Unlike personality, which is formed in solitude, character is formed in the "stream of the world"; the man of character will not avoid the herd, but will maintain "a certain integrity in the midst of the herd". Character is "armour against experience . . . not in itself deflected by experience". "From whatever direction we approach it", Read said, "we get the notion of fixity; and once a man's character is determined, it is hardly possible to speak of his moral or spiritual development . . . The emotions . . . are irrelevant to character; they are waves which break themselves in vain against its base."[7]

If character takes its origin in repression and inhibition, personality is the result of freedom and spontaneity. "The coherence of this organisation [personality]", he said, "is not to be confused with the fixed organisation of a character – any more than the coherence of a work of art is to be confused with the concision of a machine".[8] For a principle of coherence strong enough to hold the personality together and yet neither repressive nor inhibitory in nature, he turned in this book not to psychoanalysis but to literature, particularly to the French critic, Ramon Fernandez, and to Montaigne and Keats. Fernandez, he said, had found that coherence depends on a "certain inward perspective" which "does not mean that one never changes, but that the changes of the world always find you ready to select your own point of view". This conception of personality is based on "the most exact, the most complete and fearless revelation of a personality that we possess: Montaigne's Essays".

It will be seen that in both authors [Fernandez and Montaigne] we have the idea of a free disposition which is that of the sensations and memory – the sensual being – and that this being is given coherence, is defined or outlined, by a judgement which is innate. The ego is a synthesis of our sensations, is generated by conscious experience, by that inward perspective which Montaigne exercised so freely for our delectation. The judgement is not imposed on the sensations

[6] *Ibid.*, p. 13.
[7] *Ibid.*, p. 18.
[8] *Ibid.*, p. 21.

from without, as if by an external agency – that is the process of repression which results in character; judgement emerges from the history of our sensations, is elected by them, and the coherence of personality is indeed the coherence of a natural process; not the coherence of
an arbitrary discipline.[9]

In this manner Read extended the organic principle, contained
in Coleridge's distinction between 'organic' and 'mechanic' form,
to the life of the mind. The 'form' of mental and spiritual life should
accordingly be a natural growth of coherence from within the self,
not something imposed from without; an inner perspective, a
synthesis of feelings, sentiments, thoughts; a free proceeding from
within, forbidding nothing, accepting everything, and ordering it by means of a natural, innate judgment, an inner wisdom.
The 'form' of mental and spiritual life would thus be as natural
and easy a growth as the form of a plant, and held together by the
same organic coherence. The emphasis here is on inner reality, on
a delicate poise and an inner balance, not on the need for adjustment
to the harsh necessity of external reality. It is that adjustment
to the 'stream of the world' which, as Read said, produces the
fixities and angularities of character. But that world seems in
Read's view no longer real as against the reality of the self. Read's
'organic coherence' is grounded in what he called an 'illative act' –
"a belief in the existence of the self ... made possible by that
insight into the future, that belief in the continuity of experience,
which is the will to live. This is ... a state of mind very different
from that involved in character: the whole difference between
blind compulsion to an external and arbitrary ideal, and an organic
coherence intuitively based on the actual world of sensation."[10]
The reality of the self, then, becomes the essential reality for
Read. He was not interested in bringing the poetic self, the personality, to terms with external reality; the personality came to terms
with itself. Read pictured the poet in the moment of creative
activity as standing "fully conscious of the wavering confines
of his conscious mind, an expanding and contracting, a fluctuating
horizon where the light of awareness meets the darkness of oblivion".
The poet watches for lights which come "from the latent memory of
verbal images in what Freud calls the preconscious state of the mind;
or from the still obscurer state of the unconscious". The 'essential

9 *Ibid.*, pp. 23—24.
10 *Ibid.*, pp. 24—25.

faculty' at this moment, Read said, "is an awareness of one's own personality, and the capacity to cultivate its inherent activities 'without division or inner revolt' ".[11] The type of the poet, he said, is the 'mobile personality', or what Keats had called the man of 'negative capability', and not the man of character, with his "fixity of demeanour and directness of action".

This distinction between personality and character is more fundamental for Read's theory than the distinction between organic and abstract form. For his real distinction was between states of mind, and their concomitant processes of expression, rather than between kinds of form. Involved was the whole difference between 'poetry' as the expression of one mode of apprehension, and 'prose' as the expression of another. In *Form in Modern Poetry* he set forth this difference in unequivocal terms:

I believe the difference between poetry and prose to be, not one of sur-face qualities, not of form in any sense, not even of *mode* of expression, but absolutely of essence. It is not a case of the mind, in need of express-ion, choosing between two ways – one poetry, the other prose. There is no choice for the particular state of mind in which poetry originates. It must either seek poetic expression, or it must simply not be expressed; for an altogether lower tension, involving a different kind of men-tality, must be substituted before the activity of prose expression can intervene.[12]

The notion of 'personality' gave this poetic state of mind a source. To induce the state, the poet need only become aware of his person-ality and "cultivate its inherent activities, without division or inner revolt". Form, then, will follow without deliberation; the poet need not take thought on it. Read had advanced this same general view of the poetic process in "Psycho-analysis and the Critic" in 1925. But where in that essay it had been offered as an explanation of poetic inspiration, here it was made into a principle: either poetry comes about in this way, or it is simply not poetry.

There is, then, a 'true', or 'genuine' process of poetry, and a false process which Read called 'wit-writing'. He took this term from Dryden, who, he said, had described the process when he remarked that "the Composition of all poems is or ought to be of wit; and wit in the Poet, or *Wit writing* . . . is no other than the faculty of imagination in the Writer; which, like the nimble Spaniel,

[11] *Ibid.*, p. 31.
[12] *Ibid.*, p. 36.

beats over and ranges through the field of memory, till it springs the Quarry it hunted after; or, without metaphor, which searches over all the Memory for the Species or Ideas of those things which it designs to represent".[13] This describes Read's 'constructive' mode of expression, and what Dryden called 'imagination' is, in Read's terminology, 'invention'. The 'true' process of poetry, on the other hand, involved for Read not this kind of deliberate search for the right words in which to express the thought, but that 'equivalence' which we have discussed before. Here Read described it as an equation between 'intuition, or vision', on one side, and words as "isolated objective 'things' ", on the other. The words rise up into the conscious mind apparently from a preconscious or unconscious source, and they then undergo an arrangement or composition. This is not, however, the same as prose composition, because – if I understand Read rightly – the words are not USED; they function, rather, as a RELIEF for the vision.

All art originates in an act of intuition, or vision. But such *intuition* or vision must be identified with *knowledge,* being fully present only when consciously objectified. This act of vision or intuition is, physically, a state of concentration or tension in the mind. The *process* of poetry consists firstly in maintaining this vision in its integrity, and secondly in expressing this vision in words. Words are generally (that is to say, in prose) the analysis of a mental state. But in the process of poetic composition words rise into the conscious mind as isolated objective "things" with a definite equivalence in the poet's state of mental intensity. They are arranged or composed in a sequence or rhythm which is sustained until the mental state of tension in the poet is exhausted or released by this objective equivalence.[14]

Read drew a good deal of support here from the Italian critic, Leone Vivante, and some from Croce. But the basic idea, he said, went back to Vico's conception of poetry as "the primary activity of the human mind". For Read this meant that poetry itself was simply indefinable. "Poetry is properly speaking a transcendental quality – a sudden transformation which words assume under a particular influence – and we can no more define this quality than we can define a state of grace."[15]

On the basis of this distinction between a true and a false process of poetry, Read divided tradition into two antithetical parts:

[13] *Ibid.*, p. 41.
[14] *Ibid.*, pp. 39–40.
[15] *Ibid.*, p. 36.

Historically I believe that this theory of poetry is illustrated by the main tradition of English poetry which begins with Chaucer and reaches its final culmination in Shakespeare. It is contradicted by most French poetry before Baudelaire, by the so-called classical phase of English poetry culminating in Alexander Pope, and by the late Poet Laureate [Bridges]. It was reestablished in England by Wordsworth and Coleridge, developed in some degree by Browning and Gerard Manley Hopkins, and in our own day by poets like Wilfred Owen, Ezra Pound, and T. S. Eliot.[16]

Read had sketched the same 'main tradition' in *Phases of English Poetry*. In *Form in Modern Poetry*, however, he was more concerned with that part of it which began with Wordsworth and extended into modern poetry. He tried to show that, since Wordsworth, there has been a development toward a more direct – a more 'sincere' – relationship between form and the poet's state of mind. Of Wordsworth he said,

He saw, and saw rightly, that the defect of wit-writing was fundamental, and therefore to be sought in the very act of composition. He concluded that it was a *verbal* defect – and this verbal defect he identified with artificiality . . . But he was only partially right. Artificiality was only one of the symptoms of the disease. The real defect involved the state of the poet's mind in its completeness, and was reflected, not only in diction, but also throughout the whole poetic process – in modes of feeling, in diction, rhythm and metre . . . What precisely was involved was the whole theory of personality and character which I have been outlining in this essay.[17]

Between Wordsworth and the moderns, Read thought the chief figure had been Hopkins, and it was to him that he devoted most of his attention. He treated Hopkins' innovations in metrics, diction, and imagery as corollaries to his 'state of mind', and the entire discussion is punctuated by indignant complaints against "the late Poet Laureate" (Hopkins' first editor, Robert Bridges) for not having understood this. But the point is, of course, that Bridges, as a representative of the wit-writing tradition, could not have understood Hopkins in any case, and this in effect Read finally conceded: "Hopkins was a revolutionary; that is to say, his values were so fundamentally opposed to current practices that only by an effort of the imagination could they be comprehended."[18] After Hopkins came the modern poets, whose work Read

[16] *Ibid.*, p. 41.
[17] *Ibid.*, pp. 43—44.
[18] *Ibid.*, p. 48.

saw as a completion of the development begun by Wordsworth:

It was with the school which Hulme started and Pound established that the revolution begun by Wordsworth was finally completed. Diction, rhythm, and metre were fully emancipated from formal artifice, and the poet was free to act creatively under laws of his own origination. It was not always understood that, having cast off the tyranny of obsolete laws, the poet was under the necessity of originating his own, and much of the free verse that has been practised since 1914 compromises the theory by its feebleness. Nevertheless, the theory is right, and all true poetry of today, as all true poetry of the past, conforms to it. For, properly understood, this theory is not the theory of a particular school; it is the theory of all essential English poetry.[19]

2

But is the theory, in fact, adequate to account for all 'essential' English poetry, if we understand Read to mean by this the 'main tradition' which he had selected? Having divided expression into two antithetical and incompatible kinds, he had now offered a principle of form which divided the poetic self in the same way. But did this principle account for anything more than the birth of an image? One can see that it has a certain relevance to the imagist poetry written in the years just before the First World War; but can one use it to account for the work of such poets as Chaucer, Spenser, and Shakespeare in the earlier part of Read's tradition, or even for the romantic poetry of the early nineteenth century? In other words, had not Coleridge's organic principle undergone such a transformation in Read's hands as to become a different thing?

All these questions come finally to the same one: can this principle of form account for a poem as well as an image? Read was quite aware of this difficulty, and he saw correctly that if he could show his theory was adequate to account for the LONG poem he would have proved his case. Therefore he concluded his argument by going directly to the crux of the problem: how to get from essence to embodiment without breaking down his absolute distinction between two kinds of expression. "It might be objected", he said, "that whilst this theory of poetry may be accepted as a theory of poetic essence, it will not account for poetry in being, which involves, besides essence, embodiment and structure. The question

[19] *Ibid.* p. 55.

is: how can the poet pass from the metaphor and the lyric poem which is in reality no more than an extended metaphor, to those larger epic conceptions by which we measure the greatness of poets?"[20]

Now to answer this question, Read had really only two alternatives. He could conceive the long poem as being poetry only in places and not throughout its entire length. Or he could conceive it as being continuously poetry, in which case he would have to account for its structure and organization as products of the poetic state of mind. The first of these alternatives is the one he had apparently embraced in *English Prose Style* when he said, "Prose is a structure of ready-made words. Its 'creative' function is confined to plan and elevation – functions these too of Poetry, but in Poetry subsidiary to the creative function."[21] This would seem to assign a characteristic prose function, 'plan and elevation', to poetry, but only in a subsidiary role. The first alternative was also the one taken by Coleridge. "A poem of any length", he said, "neither can be, nor ought to be, all poetry. Yet if an harmonious whole is to be produced, the remaining parts must be preserved in keeping with the poetry; and this can be no otherwise effected than by such a studied selection and artificial arrangement, as will partake of one, though not a peculiar property of poetry. And this . . . can be no other than the property of exciting a more continuous and equal attention than the language of prose aims at, whether colloquial or written."[22] But Read, unlike Coleridge, had no way of distinguishing between 'poetry', as a mental activity, and 'poems', as a product of art. For him, there were simply two states of mind, one expressed in poetry and the other in prose; and because of the nature of these states, a "studied selection and artificial arrangement" could go on only in the prose process, not in the poetic: there could be an 'art' of prose but not of poetry. Thus, whatever he may have meant in *English Prose Style* by proposing 'plan and elevation' as a subsidiary poetic function, in *Form in Modern Poetry* Read rejected the first alternative. It meant, he said, "that there is 'pure poetry,' and that the rest is prose, or padding".[23]

[20] *Ibid.*, p. 55.
[21] See above, p. 64.
[22] S. T. Coleridge, *Biographia Literaria*, ed. J. Shawcross (London, 1907), Vol. II, p. 11.
[23] *Form in Modern Poetry*, p. 60.

Read chose to conceive the structural and organizational elements of a poem as products of the poetic state of mind, and therefore he had to show that there is a poetic kind of organization different from the kind that obtains in prose. He did this – if I understand him rightly – in the same way he had made "thought' poetic: by effecting a transmutation whereby the organizational elements become visual and emotional. I will give the essentials of his rather involved and circuitous argument. The distinction between the lyric and the long poem, he held, is that the former is dominated by an emotion and the latter by an idea. "We might define the lyric as a poem which embodies a single or simple emotional attitude, a poem which expresses directly an uninterrupted mood or inspiration. A long poem, it would follow as a corollary, is one which unites by artifice several or many such emotional moods; though here the artifice might imply a single dominating *idea* which in itself might be an emotional unity."[24] The lyric and the long poem, he said, are organized in different ways: emotion leads to 'form', or 'structure'; idea leads to 'conception', or 'invention'. And it is these organizational elements which lead us out of the narrow impasse of 'pure' poetry:

What the advocate of "pure" poetry is defining is not poetry, but only a species of poetry, namely, "pure" poetry. Let us admit, even, that word-music, image and metaphor are the blood-stream of poetry, without which it cannot for a moment exist. Yet beyond these are structure and conception – structure which is the embodiment of words in a pattern or form; and conception, which is the projection of the poet's thought into a process from which, or during the course of which, words are generated.

That is to say, there can be no words with their accompanying music, no images with their visual immediacy, no metaphors with their more-than-verbal meaning, unless there is either an intuition of form, which I take to be an emotion about fitness, size, appropriateness, tension, tautness and so on (as in the sonnet); or, not alternatively so much as in addition, a progressive invention which will carry the poet on from word to word, line to line, stanza to stanza, book to book, until the invention is exhausted.[25]

The difference between a long and short poem, he said, lies in the way these two elements, form and conception, are related. When the temporal process of conception occurs with the forming process in a single creative act, the resulting poem is a lyric; when it is

[24] *Ibid.*, p. 57.
[25] *Ibid.*, pp. 60—61.

not so fused and form is dependent on the working-out of conception, the result is a long poem:

Form and conception are present in the lyric, but they are unobtrusive; the duration of the poetry is so short, the emotion so immediate (and relatively simple) that we do not perceive (it is the poet's business to conceal) the time-structure. Form and conception are fused in the act of creation. When form dominates the conception (that is to say, when the conception is limited enough to be seen as a single unit – to be held from the beginning to the end in one mental tension), then the poem can be defined properly as "short". On the other hand, when the conception is so complex that the mind must take it in in disjointed series, finally ordering these series in a comprehensive unity, then the poem is properly defined as "long".[26]

These distinctions between the short and long poem seem generally acceptable. The difficulty comes with Read's refusal to acknowledge what appears so evident: that the complex conception of a long poem is, in his terms, actually 'constructive', not 'creative'. The logic of his argument forced him instead to insist that the 'artifice' by means of which the long poem becomes a unity is of a wholly different order from prose artifice. Keats, he said, had called the long poem "a test of Invention which I take to be the Polar Star of poetry . . ." .But Keats, he thought, had failed in his own long poems because he had merely decorated his narrative with imagery and so had impeded its course. "His poems may be compared with motor-cars moving slowly in procession at a Carnival of Flowers, which must be stripped of their lovely decorations before they can resume their proper speed."[27] The poet must not hang decorations on his narrative in this manner; instead he must VISUALIZE his narrative. "The poet will be poetically inspired by the narrative to the extent that he visualizes the events of the narrative, and is moved by the visualization. He will be moved so long as, in the famous phrase, he keeps his eye on the objects, on the visualized events."[28] Similarly, the philosophical poem must be made visual. "We may doubt whether the totality of a system, or any purely philosophic theme, can be made the subject of a poem (necessarily a long poem) unless it is translated into action or imagery . . . . Poetry of any length is visual or it is tedious; it may

[26] *Ibid.*, p. 61.
[27] *Ibid.*, p. 67.
[28] *Ibid.*, p. 68.

be visual by virtue of its action, or by virtue of its imagery. It can never, whilst still remaining poetry, be merely informative or conceptual."[29] If, in other words, the long poem merely narrates or informs, its invention remains prosaic; if, however, the story or the idea is visualized, the invention becomes poetic. But does it thereby differ from prose invention in the sense of being an expression of an altogether different state of mind? Has Read in this way overcome the time element between conception and form in the long poem, an element that belongs properly to 'constructive', or 'prose' expression? Does 'thought' in the long poem become 'word' instantaneously, as it does in the lyric where form and conception are fused in a single act?

Read, at any rate, believed that it does. He evidently assumed that by transforming invention into something visual, he had removed it to the level of poetic apprehension, where 'thought' is instantaneous, non-conceptual, emotional. He insisted that the organizational elements of the long poem are different in kind from their counterparts in prose:

... I think it is dangerous to admit, as Mr. Lascelles Abercrombie does in *The Idea of Great Poetry*, that the far richer and greater effects of the long poem can be achieved "by means of a unity far less direct", and "a form less immediately impressive and, therefore, no doubt, less lovely" than the means employed in a successful sonnet. There are really no degrees of poetry; at least, there is no easy transition from poetry to prose. The two forms of expression are distinct in kind, we must speak in either one mode or the other. It is not enough even to be "visual"; prose can be "visual". Poetry must be visual in a swift, intuitive way. It must also, by its daring, adventure into a world of sense and sound beyond the reach of the mundane instruments of prose. That is its faculty of Invention, about which Keats speaks. Invention and Imagery – Poetry is an essence distilled by these emotional activities. But it is not an essence which we can dilute with the water of prose, to make it go a long way. There are many varieties of poetic expression, just as there are many voices that sing; but none of them forgoes its proper harmony.[30]

This means that the two terms EMOTION and IDEA, which Read had proposed as the basis for his distinction between the lyric and the long poem, issue at the end of his argument into two 'emotional activities', Imagery and Invention. In this way, poetic invention

[29] *Ibid.*, p. 71.
[30] *Ibid.*, pp. 71—72.

becomes "distinct in kind" from prosaic invention, reaching
a "world of sense and sound" closed to prose. Read had begun by
defining the long poem as "one which unites by artifice several or
many . . . emotional moods; though here the artifice might imply
a single dominating idea which in itself might be an emotional
unity". We can see now that this 'artifice' is not meant to be the
artifice of prose expression: the 'single dominating idea' IS the
artifice, and the 'emotional unity' IS the idea.

I do not think this will work. Read's theory is actually a theory
of the lyric – even more narrowly, of the image – and nothing
more. To account for form in a modern poetry which had abandoned
all conventional and arbitrary forms, he had appropriated Coleridge's
notion of organic form. Coleridge, Read said at one point in his
argument, "defined the principle of modern poetry in these words:
'No work of true genius dares want its appropriate form, neither is
there any danger of this. As it must not, so genius can not, be lawless
for it is even this that constitutes its genius – *the power of acting
creatively under laws of its own origination.*' " Read went on to say,
"By 'modern' poetry I mean all genuine poetry from his own day
to ours – and indeed all genuine poetry of all time."[31] Now Coleridge
may have stated the principle of modern poetry, and indeed of
all poetry, in this celebrated phrase; but Read had narrowed
the application of it to that inexplicable moment in the poetic
process when 'thought' becomes 'word' – the moment when an
'exact' objective equivalence wells up from the poet's 'personality'.
This was for Read the real process of poetry, and it was this process
which he believed modern poets had brought to a new state of
refinement. Read's poetic theory was therefore inescapably a
theory of the single creative moment. He could join a number of
these moments together in a series, but in that case the thread,
or cement, had to be accounted for. By making it emotional
and visual, he had tried to make it 'creative' in the same sense
the 'moments' themselves were creative. I cannot see, however,
that he had overcome in any convincing fashion the problem of
the time-interval between conception and form in the long poem;
that he had succeeded in showing poetic artifice to be a different
KIND of artifice from prose artifice. The emotion behind it might
be more intense, more impelling; the problems of composition and

[31] *Ibid.*, p. 35.

arrangement might therefore be solved more rapidly; but that is as far as one can go, I think, without having the poem, as poem, vanish from the theory. Read's principle of organic form could not encompass the long poem.

Coleridge's, on the other hand, could and did. Unlike Read, Coleridge had been able to distinguish 'poems' from 'poetry'. He had first discriminated poems from works of science on the basis of their different ends, and poems, from what we would call prose fiction on the basis of their different means. He had then identified poetry with a mental activity which he called the Imagination, a 'synthetic and magical power' which operates by means of the reconciliation of opposites.[32] What Read called the 'creative' and 'constructive' modes of expression were for Coleridge balanced and reconciled in the poetic process, and thus he could consider as a part of organic form those elements of the work of art which are contributed by the conscious and deliberate working of the mind. Read's notion of imagination, however, was far narrower than Coleridge's. It was confined, according to what he had said in *English Prose Style* and *Phases of English Poetry*, to the mysterious process by which an image becomes an 'equivalent' for an idea or an emotion — "the act or moment of creative thought", "the birth of the image or the word".

Essence and embodiment. How to get from the one to the other was the central theoretical problem for Read. He could no more admit rational construction into the poetic act than he could admit the discursive reason into that 'direct awareness' of unity which was for him poetic apprehension. He could only try to establish a principle of form so deep within the poet's psyche that rational construction could be dispensed with, or at best regarded as mere embroidery and embellishment. Yet, even so, he could not account for much more than the single image emerging from the single creative act. Only by maintaining that this same image could, in effect, be a long poem — a poem as long, even, as *The Faerie Queene* — could he encompass with his theory the tradition of 'true' poetry which he had selected. His distinction between absolutely different kinds of cognition and of expression had led him into an impasse. There was no way out. He could only proceed farther away from the poem and deeper into the psyche of the poet.

[32] Coleridge, *op. cit.*, pp. 10—12.

PART TWO

THE REHABILITATION OF ROMANTICISM

VI

"CLASSICAL" AND "ROMANTIC"

1

In the years following the publication of *Form in Modern Poetry*, Read set out to 'rehabilitate' romanticism. Just as the poet, in Read's view, stood face-to-face with his 'personality', cultivating its inherent activities "without division or inner revolt", so in criticism Read stood face-to-face with the 'night-side' of the mind, with the intimate, internal world on the other side of consciousness, convinced that from this anarchic region of feeling, emotion, instinct, impulse and dream, true order issues. By the end of the 1930's he had worked out a neo-romanticism under which the rational mode was altogether abandoned: sympathy became criticism, the dream became the poem, anarchy became order.

To embark on such a program of 'rehabilitation', however, Read needed to establish his critical terminology, particularly the terms 'classical' and 'romantic'. The term 'classical', as Read used it during the early 1920's, had more often than not connotations of 'good', and 'romantic' of 'bad'. When, therefore, he began to establish modern poetry as 'romantic', he had to shift his terms in such a way that 'romantic' became 'good' and 'classical' became 'bad'. To track these terms through Read's writings, and to make complete sense of his use of them, seems nearly impossible. They occur frequently, in many contexts, and with apparently many meanings. Yet the way their connotations shifted between 'good' and 'bad' is significant, and I will attempt to explain here how this shift took place.

In the 1920's, Read had used the term 'romantic' generally to mean 'sentimental', referring to an art of loose emotion and flowing subjectivity; and he had used 'classical' to refer to a formal and patterned art of intellectual order and control. Much of the time he had seemed to be well within the 'tendency' which Eliot said the *Criterion* represented: toward "something that may be called classicism"; toward "a higher and clearer conception of the Reason, and a more severe and serene control of the emotions by Reason".[1] Yet there had been differences. Read's antiromanticism, for example, had been directed at what he called 'sentimental' romanticism – which seemed to mean the poetry of the later nineteenth century – and seldom at any of the romantic poets of the earlier part of the century. Above all, he had never been ready to give up Wordsworth.

His distinction between romanticism and classicism, moreover, was fundamentally psychological, and was influenced to a considerable extent, I think, by his work in art criticism, particularly by the ideas of the art historian, Wilhelm Worringer. Worringer had explained the appearance of representational and non-representational styles in the history of art as the result of a changing 'will-to-form'. Thus abstract styles revealed a feeling of shyness and withdrawal before the flux of nature and a desire for transcendence over it through the use of geometrical forms; representational styles revealed a feeling of organic harmony with nature. Worringer called the one 'will-to-form' *abstraktion* and the other *einfühlung*. The general effect of his distinction was to justify abstraction as a legitimate artistic expression; and since nineteenth century art had become academic in its development of representational styles, Worringer's rationale for abstraction undoubtedly was influential in shifting taste. It was used by T. E Hulme, who introduced Worringer's ideas in England, to justify the formalist tendencies of the new art and poetry. But Hulme incorporated it into his own militantly anti-romantic program, and used it as part of the rationale for what he called a new 'classical' movement in the arts (despite the fact that Worringer's *abstraktion* was a will-to-form exactly opposite to that revealed in the organic, empathic art of classical antiquity).[2] Perhaps Read first learned of Worringer's ideas through Hulme's writings, when he edited them after the war.[3] At any rate, these ideas, as Read used them in his art criticism

[1] T. S. Eliot, "The Idea of a Literary Review", *Criterion*, IV. 1 (1926), 5.

[2] Worringer's basic thesis is set forth in *Abstraction and Empathy* (London, 1953). The influence of this thesis on Hulme can be seen in his "Modern Art and its Philosophy", "Humanism and the Religious Attitude", and "Romanticism and Classicism", in *Speculations*. For critical studies of this influence, see Joseph Frank's "Spatial Form in Modern Literature", *loc. cit.*, and Frank Kermode's *Romantic Image*.

[3] An English translation of Worringer's *Abstraktion und Einfühlung* did not appear until 1953, and Hulme's abstract of Worringer's thesis in "Mo-

during the 1920's, sometimes carried the anti-romantic stamp which Hulme had given them. The abstract tendency, that is, appeared as 'classical', and the empathic, organic tendency as 'romantic'. And there was no doubt that for the most part Read preferred periods in the history of art in which the 'abstract' tendency had been dominant.[4] Thus in his art criticism we can find an 'organic' – 'abstract' polarity in which 'abstract' has connotations of 'good' and 'organic' of 'bad'.

What particularly appealed to him was the possibility of relating abstract form in art to philosophical abstractions, as different expressions of the same tendency. He saw, for example, Gothic art as an exact parallel to the metaphysical abstractions of medieval philosophy.

When religious emotion is ... given a *formal* value, we may have as a result two kinds of expression determined respectively by the sensational and by the intellectual content of the mind: one is a universal type of art which we call classical or hieratic; the other is the art of philosophy in its widest sense, including metaphysics.[5]

In this way Read interpreted Worringer's ideas to mean that the artist's aesthetic abstractions are a kind of alternative expression to the philosopher's conceptual abstractions. Now, this notion carried over to some extent into his poetic theory. The poetic equivalent of the artist's abstract form seems to be what Read called 'metaphysical' poetry. The tendency toward an organic, empathic relationship with the environment was manifested in what he called 'lyrical' poetry. We can find the same polarity, that is, in poetry as in the visual arts. And although he did not designate 'metaphysical' poetry as 'classical', he did call 'lyrical' poetry 'romantic'.

In general, we can say that the terms 'classical' and 'romantic', as Read often used them in the 1920's had little to do with historical periods of classicism and romanticism. They indicated, rather,

---

dern Art and its Philosophy" long remained one of the chief sources of Worringer's ideas to non-German readers in England. Read edited the translation of Worringer's *Form in Gothic* (London, 1927), and contributed a preface in which he quoted extensively from Hulme's abstract.

[4] See *English Stained Glass*, and *The Meaning of Art* (London, 1931).

[5] *English Stained Glass*, p. 18. In the preface Read expressed his indebtedness to Worringer, "of whose ideas I confess myself an enthusiastic devotee".

a tendency toward formality and abstraction, or a tendency toward the expression of empathy and emotion. They seem, indeed, to be no more than what we have previously called formalism and expressionism, the two poles which Read's theory always attempts to reconcile and harmonize. Thus both 'classical' and 'romantic' tendencies appeared to him to be legitimate and necessary, although either (and particularly the 'romantic') could be carried to excess. He saw an opposition between them, which went on even within the mind of the artist. He found, he said in "Psychoanalysis and Criticism", "a peculiar echo of reality in these words of André Gide":

It is important to remember that the struggle between classicism and romanticism also exists inside each mind. And it is from this very struggle that the work is born; the classic work of art relates the triumph of order and measure over an inner romanticism. And the wilder the riot to be tamed the more beautiful your work will be. If the thing is orderly in its inception, the work will be cold and without interest.[6]

Read's anti-romanticism was really an objection to a loosely emotional art in which this balance was not achieved. He wanted 'emotion' channelled and restrained by 'reason', subjectivity controlled and shaped in the objectivity of form. The title of his first book of literary criticism, *Reason and Romanticism*, expressed this notion of an opposition between two vital forces which is harmonized in the work of art. When this harmony was attained, Read was ready to praise the artist, whether he be nominally romantic or classical. His highest praise, indeed, was reserved for the romantic artist when he maintained perfect control over the most tempestuous of passions. In the work of Charlotte Bronte, for example, he found "emotion in subjection – the very definition of art !"[7] And he held that *Wuthering Heights*, "with its unerring unity of conception and its full catharsis of the emotions of pity and terror, is one of the few occasions on which the novel has reached the dignity of classical tragedy".[8] Whether an artist were romantic or classical was for Read really beside the point. It was rather a matter of the artist's natural disposition, his extraversion or introversion, and he thought that

[6] "Psychoanalysis and Criticism", *Reason and Romanticism*, p. 93.
[7] "Charlotte and Emily Bronte", *Reason and Romanticism*, p. 182.
[8] *Ibid.*, p. 184.

the critic, like the psychologist, should take up a position above the conflict, and although his own psychological state may lead him to sympathize with one school or the other, yet as a scientific critic he must no longer be content with a dog-in-the-manger attitude ... He must see the romantic and classic elements in literature as the natural expression of a biological opposition in human nature. It is not sufficient to treat the matter one way or the other as a question of intellectual fallacy; it is a question, for the individual, of natural necessity ....[9]

Read went on to identify the romantic with extraversion and the classicist with introversion: "You will find . . . that the romantic artist always expresses some function of the extraverted attitude, whilst the classic artist always expresses some function of the introverted attitude."[10] I think he was led to this rather surprising identification (which he later reversed) because he was following Jung here. We saw earlier how in this same essay he had been attracted to Jung's notion of 'phantasy' – a psychic activity which unites subject and object, thought and feeling, idea and thing – as the basic creative act.[11] But for Jung there are differences in the way this activity takes place, since there are two fundamental psychological types, extravert and introvert, determined – as Read explained – "according to whether the general mental energy of the individual is directed outwards to the visible, actual world, or inward to the world of thought and imagery". This means that there are two types of artist, whose art shows characteristic differences. Thus Jung had identified introversion with Worringer's aesthetic category, *abstraktion* – a withdrawal from the flow of reality to the security of geometric forms; and extraversion with *einfühlung* – a trust and confidence in the flow and a delight in organic forms.[12] To Read, then, for whom the tendency toward abstraction appeared at this time to be 'classical', the introverted artist would naturally seem to be the classicist.

Read's 'classicism', then, was from the beginning a very individual thing. It appears to have been based almost entirely on his formalist tastes and his reaction against sentimental and academic nineteenth-

[9] "Psychoanalysis and Criticism", *loc. cit.*, p. 104.

[10] *Ibid.* He was not, however, consistent in this identification. Elsewhere in *Reason and Romanticism* he regarded the classic artist generally as the extravert, *e.g.*, Smollet and Jane Austen.

[11] See above, p. 58;

[12] C. G. Jung, *Psychological Types* (London, 1924), p. 358. This book was Read's source for his discussion of introversion and extraversion.

century art. Far from being genuinely anti-romantic, he regarded romanticism as a normal and valuable psychological tendency without which the opposed classical tendency would be sterile. During most of the 1920's, he seems to have maintained an attitude sufficiently 'classical' to make him acceptable to Eliot and the *Criterion*, but also romantic enough to make his position always somewhat uncertain.

2

Sometime in the early 1920's Read evidently decided to establish a set of critical terms to accord with his new views, and until these terms finally became established in the mid-1930's, his progress was most confusing to follow. Parts of *Form in Modern Poetry* were published in journals in 1931; yet as late as April, 1931, he was still calling himself a classicist:

My own preferences are classical: that is to say, I derive most pleasure from a work of art, whether literature or painting, in which expression is achieved with some degree of formal precision. But I could never see why, though a classicist, I should be forbidden the enjoyment of romantic art.[13]

And the year before he had published a pamphlet, *Julien Benda and the New Humanism*, in which Benda was held up as a foe of romanticism and apostle of post-war classicism. Benda, he said, had performed the task of destroying the 'literary Bergsonians', if not Bergson himself.

The cult of vagueness, the musicalization of all the arts, the general subjectivism and romanticism of modern art, the palpitating pan-lyricism that distinguished so much pre-war literature – M. Benda fell foul of these and held up for our admiration the contrasted ideals of order, clarity, and precision . . . More than any other book [Belphegor] has been the rallying-point of classicism in modern criticism.[14]

In this pamphlet Read appeared to be speaking from an anti-romantic and anti-humanist position much like that of Hulme or Eliot. He attacked Norman Foerster and the American humanists,

---

[13] Quoted by H. W. Haüsermann, *loc. cit.*, p. 72, from *The Listener* (April 16, 1931), 679.

[14] *Julien Benda and the New Humanism*, p. 14.

for example, for presuming to construct a humanism without recognizing an 'absolute severance' of the human and the absolute.

I cling close to Spinoza's dictum and feel that there is no bridging the gap between the finite and the infinite. With T. E. Hulme, who in this matter is so closely echoed by M. Benda, I hold that most of our errors spring from an attempt on our part to gloze over and disguise a particular discontinuity in the nature of reality.[15]

Read pointed out that since the American humanists had no absolute standards to fall back upon, they could only find their standards in man himself. He seemed to be still quite firmly in Eliot's camp. Four years earlier, Eliot had praised him for searching for "something outside". The issue, Eliot had said, is between those who

make *man the measure of all things*, and those who would find an extra-human measure. There are those who find this measure in a revealed religion, and those who, like Mr. Irving Babbitt and Mr. Read, look for it without pretending to have found it.[16]

Yet less than two years after his pamphlet on Benda appeared, Read in *Form in Modern Poetry* introduced his notion of 'personality' through which he seemed to be searching more 'inside' than 'outside' for his standard.

Neither Read nor anyone else has furnished a satisfactory explanation of this metamorphosis of 'classical' into 'romantic'. Fishman remarked in his study of Read, "It is not easy to explain how the admiration of logic, structure, and order so manifest in *Reason and Romanticism* was completely transformed in Read's aesthetic speculations."[17] Although I feel just as puzzled over some aspects of the change, I am convinced at least of one thing: it was not Read's admiration for order that was transformed, but the nature of the order he admired. Where in *Reason and Romanticism* order had been (or seemed to be) intellectual, by the late 1920's it had become aesthetic. Thus the 'absolutes' to which he proclaimed his adherence at this time were – although he did not always say so – fundamentally aesthetic. We can see this very clearly, for example, in an essay on behaviorism published in 1928. Read called

---

[15] *Ibid.*, p. 42.

[16] T. S. Eliot, review of *Reason and Romanticism*, *Criterion*, IV. 4 (1926), 755.

[17] S. Fishman, "Sir Herbert Read: Poetics vs. Criticism", *loc. cit.*, 158.

upon the behaviorists to recognize the existence of objective values which could be apprehended intuitively. But 'value' here was Whiteheadian 'pattern'. "By *value*, in ethics", Read said, "I mean a sum of the activities in any line of conduct resulting in a pattern or definite arrangement of a set of particulars which in itself and for its own sake we can contemplate as an end or being." He said this may be "merely an apprehension of the *aesthetic* form or configuration of a given abstraction". "By *intuition*", he said, "I mean 1) the perception of a pattern of this kind, and 2) the simultaneous perception of the relation of such a pattern to the universal order."[18] It is this sudden perception of a plane of value that Read has elsewhere called 'the sense of glory'.[19] Yet it is certainly to be doubted that such an intuitively apprehended 'pattern' is the 'something outside' which Eliot had praised Read for seeking. Read could call it 'objective', but the term is actually irrelevant here, as is the term 'subjective'. For behind this notion of value as 'pattern' is Whitehead's doctrine of 'connectedness', by means of which the subjective-objective distinction is overthrown and subjects become objects and objects subjects.[20] And since Read conceives value from this point of view, he has never had to give up the notion of 'absolutes'.[21]

[18] "The Implications of Behaviorism", *Criterion*, VII, 4 (1928), 75.

[19] "Glory may be only one form of romanticism; but so is every kind of idealism. Romanticism, whether we like it or not, is always with us. But though we cannot escape from romanticism, we can discriminate between the multiplicity of sentiments to which it gives rise, introducing among those sentiments an order whose integrity is this very sense of glory." – from "Prefatory Note" to *The Sense of Glory*. "At certain moments the individual is carried beyond his rational self, onto another ethical plane, where his actions are judged by new standards. The impulse which moves him to irrational action I have called the sense of glory. . . ." – *Annals of Innocence and Experience*, p. 229.

[20] See A. N. Whitehead, *Modes of Thought*, p. 13.

[21] Read concluded his argument in *Form in Modern Poetry* by attempting to link up the 'personality' with a 'realm of essence'. He said (p. 78): "The whole structure, not merely of this particular theory of poetry, but of the philosophy of life on which it is based, would fall to pieces unless related to a belief in what Santayana has called a realm of essence; the highest poetry is inconceivable without the intuition of pure Being as well as the sense of existence. Art is empty unless it can glimpse perfection." Read did not explain any further the nature of this 'realm of essence', but, considering his argument as a whole in this book, it seems to me that it can only be an aesthetic realm of 'pattern'.

Thus by the late 1920's (if not before), Read's 'classicism' had become in a very fundamental sense aesthetic formalism. For not only was his preference in the arts for the formal and the patterned, but the absolutes to which he adhered were themselves 'form' and 'pattern'. What happened in the early 1930's, I think, was that he discovered he could no longer call the formalist tendency 'classical'. He saw art as the synthesis in a dialectic between inner and outer reality, a synthesis which showed characteristic differences according to the introverted or extraverted predisposition of the artist. These differences appeared as a tendency toward formalism, which he called 'classicism', or 'reason'; and a tendency toward expressionism, which he called 'romanticism', or 'emotion'. But he had made a distinction in kind between the rational and the poetic modes of cognition, and between these two modes there was no dialectic: poetry, that is, was the product of 'creative' expression alone, not a synthesis of the 'creative' and 'constructive' modes. Insofar as art was concerned, therefore, the synthesis between inner and outer reality did not involve the rational mode at all. It was wholly the product of intuition, of the 'personality', of an inward direction of mental energy. The formalist and expressionist tendencies, therefore, functioned within the one 'intuitional-creative' mode, and the formalist tendency had no relation to the 'rational-constructive' mode. Thus it became increasingly difficult for Read to call the formalist tendency 'classical' and at the same time to keep it distinct from the 'constructive' mode of expression which had historically been involved in the production of so much classical and neo-classical art. The only solution was to line up all his terms along the 'creative' – 'constructive' dichotomy.

3

In *Form in Modern Poetry* Read's new terminology began to emerge. He proposed here, as we have seen, a distinction between two kinds of poetic form, 'organic' and 'abstract', to go with his distinction between two modes of expression and two traditions of poetry. And since his argument was intended to establish modern poetry as a continuation or completion of the revolution begun by Wordsworth, it was essential that he extricate it from the anti-romantic critical milieu in which it had developed. He could do this only by abandoning the particular meanings the terms 'romantic' and 'classical' had acquired under post-war classicism, and pinning those terms to historical periods of romanticism and classicism. This was not easy, in view of his own 'classical' past, and in the first pages of *Form in Modern Poetry* he struggled unhappily with what he called "these confusing terms". It was his experience as a poet, he said, that made the organic-abstract distinction necessary.

When . . . a critic-poet attempts to probe down into such a fundamental question as the form and structure of poetry, he cannot escape the evidence of his own experience, but must in some way establish an agreement between his theory and his practice.[22]

Without such experiences, he said, his own theory "most definitely" would have been classical. "But when I stand up squarely to the traditional terms of classical theory, and attempt to relate them to my experience, I find there is no application – my experience cuts across the classical-romantic categorisation."[23] He proceeded, however, to say that the distinction between organic and abstract form could be

directly related to the concepts "romantic" and " classical," provided these concepts are accepted in their proper, that is to say, their *historical* sense . . .. The transition from the organic type to the abstract always coincides with the transition from a period of stress and energy to a period of satiety and solidity; and that is the historical distinction between romantic and classical periods, and it is quite clear that the classical and romantic periods are related to each other in a "life cycle" which is the recurring cycle of growth, maturity, and decay of culture.[24]

Now, this concept of alternating historical periods of romantic 'stress and energy' and classical 'satiety and solidity' should not be confused with Worringer's concept of two 'wills-to-form' manifesting themselves in the history of art. This new distinction was between the vitality of a form while the creative impulse is still fresh, and the sterility of the same form when the impulse is dead and the form becomes a pattern mechanically repeated. Read used an example from Scythian art which makes this clear. Early Scythian ornamentation, he said,

[22] *Form in Modern Poetry*, pp. 1—2.
[23] *Ibid.*, p. 2.
[24] *Ibid.*, p. 4. Read acknowledged his indebtedness here to Sir Herbert Grierson's definitions of the terms "classical" and "romantic".

usually took the shape of very vigorous and lively representations of animals . . .. The designs were generally stylised; that is to say, the natural form of the animal was distorted in the interests of linear rhythm and dynamic effect. The form of such objects I should describe as organic; every departure from truth-to-nature is at the same time an intensification of natural vitality.[25]

In later Scythian art, however, the same forms were used in 'stereotyped combinations':

The form is abstracted from the original impulse and made to serve as a unit in an arrangement which is not related to the original impulse, but is an abstract (numerical) arrangement of given units.[26]

The distinction, then, is between 'vital' and 'mechanical', in Coleridge's sense, or, as Read was later to term it, between art 'properly so-called' and 'academic' art. Thus this distinction cuts across the other distinction between two psychological tendencies, 'abstraction' and 'empathy' – either of which could be, in Read's sense, an 'original impulse' – and it carries with it the terms 'romantic' and 'classical'.

Even so, to remove the unfavorable connotations that had come to surround 'romantic' was difficult and required some juggling of terms:

I wish to avoid these confusing terms [classical and romantic] as much as possible, though I think no confusion is necessary if we bear in mind the two distinct meanings of each term. In one case we can distinguish the meanings verbally, for "classical" may be reserved for the historical sense, whilst "classicistic" serves for the derivative and sentimental sense; and perhaps we ought to be bold enough to use "romanticistic" as well as "romantic". . . . It is most important to remember that the term "romantic" especially is often restricted to an art based on sentiment, which may be typical of inferior classical as well as of inferior romantic periods. To be quite clear, when referring to this type of romanticism, we might always call it "sentimental-romanticism."[27]

He seemed here to be allowing genuinely classical art some status as art, but the logical end of his series of distinctions was of course to make the difference between 'romantic' and 'classical' absolute, in line with his distinction between 'creative' and 'constructive' expression. In *English Prose Style*, where he had proposed this distinction, he had said:

[25] *Ibid.*, pp. 2—3.
[26] *Ibid.*, p. 3.
[27] *Ibid.*, p. 4.

The predominance which is given on the one hand to order or judgment and on the other to emotion or feeling determines those opposed types of expression which are given the historical terms "classical" or "romantic". The *priority* of either of these qualities determines the distinction between prose and poetry.[28]

And he had then added in a footnote, "The difference between romanticism and classicism is therefore one of degree; between prose and poetry it is one of kind."[29] In the revised edition of this book (New York, 1952) that footnote is omitted, for it is precisely as one of kind, not of degree, that Read has come to see the difference between romanticism and classicism. This distinction, since the mid-1930's, has been the same as that between 'prose' and 'poetry', *i.e.*, absolute. In 1932, however, he was apparently not quite ready for this step. Indeed, he seemed a little chary of becoming identified as a romanticist, because of the common association of the term with that 'sentimental-romanticism' from which he wished at all costs to remain dissociated. He concluded his book by saying:

There is not one literary tradition, but many traditions; there is certainly a romantic tradition as well as a classical tradition, and, if anything, the romantic tradition has the longer history . . . . If we must apply the historical distinctions to this age of ours, we shall find ourselves in a dilemma, for we shall be forced to admit that whilst it is possibly an age of satiety, it is not one of solidity; and if it is certainly an age of stress, we are more doubtful about its energy. That is to say, it is not clearly either a romantic or a classical age, nor are the categories of a romantic or a classical tradition applicable to it. In the circumstances the poet has no alternative but to rely on "a certain inward perspective", a coherence of the personality based on the widest evidence of the senses.[30]

4

After 1932, Read's critical terminology tended to form two distinct clusters. One was composed of the terms, 'rational-constructive-classical-abstract-character-extraversion'; the other of 'intuitional creative-romantic-organic-personality-introversion'. And each cluster attracted other terms to it, so that we can compile a long list

[28] *English Prose Style* (London, 1928), p. 154.
[29] *Ibid.*
[30] *Form in Modern Poetry*, p. 81.

of such antithetical pairs from Read's writings. I will have more to say later about the relationship between the two cognitive modes around which the clusters were formed; for the present, however, it should be noted again that art is the product of a dialectical opposition between inner and outer reality which does not involve the rational mode. Therefore, some of the terms previously used to designate the formalist tendency which had appeared to associate it with the rational mode had now to be shifted. Thus 'classical' was placed in the rational cluster, as was 'abstract' (at least as it related to poetic form).[31] 'Introversion', on the other hand, was placed in the intuitional cluster to go with 'personality', which meant that it lost its association with 'classical' and 'abstract'.

When Read revised some of his earlier writings, he shifted terms where necessary to bring them into accord with his mature views, and the consequence was often a bewildering difference between early and late versions of the same work. For example, the sentence in 'Psychoanalysis and Criticism'' in which he identified introversion with classicism and extraversion with romanticism appeared in *Collected Essays* with the identification exactly reversed: "You will find . . . that the romantic artist always expresses some function of the introverted attitude, whilst the classic artist always expresses some function of the extraverted attitude."[32] A similar change occurred when he revised *English Prose Style*. In 1928 he had used a scholastic distinction between "an internal and external direction of the will" which he called, respectively, 'Thought' and 'Sensibility', and which he identified rather loosely with introversion and extraversion. When he then joined four 'modes of operation' to the two categories, Thought and Sensibility, the result was a table of eight possible 'types of rhetoric'. In the revised edition of the book he abandoned this table for one derived from Jung's psychological types and functions. The category Thought

[31] Read continued to use 'abstract' to designate the formalist tendency in the plastic arts. In relation to these arts, then, the term is still 'good', and should not be confused with 'abstract form' in poetry, which, with its opposite, 'organic form', helps make up the two dichotomous clusters of terms. Read said in *Annals* (pp. 218—219): "Romanticism is not essentially a formal question . . . The constructive movement in modern architecture, sculpture and painting is . . . of a formal purity not excelled in any classical period; and yet it is an essentially romantic art, or I would not have spent so much of my energy in its defence."

[32] *Collected Essays*, p. 144.

was replaced by one called Extraversion, and Sensibility by Introversion. Thus the inward and outward directions were exactly reversed, and some of the types of rhetoric that in 1928 were the product of an inward direction became the product of an outward direction.[33] All this came about, I think, because the term 'introversion' was put into the cluster with 'romantic' and 'personality'. (There were many other changes in *English Prose Style*. One, worth noting, was the deletion of a distinction made in 1928 between 'character' and 'personality' which made 'character' the superior type.[34])

Read reprinted most of *Form in Modern Poetry*, with only minor changes, in *Collected Essays*. When, however, he came to the last paragraph, in which he had ended by saying that ours is "not clearly either a romantic or a classical age", and that "the poet has no alternative but to rely on 'a certain inward perspective'", he added this concluding sentence:

I am aware that I shall be accused of merely dressing up the old romanticism in new phrases; but forced into this academic discussion I might then accept "the rehabilitation of romanticism" as an adequate description of my aims.[35]

No longer was he reluctant to be identified as a romanticist. But by the time this sentence was added, the 'rehabilitation' was already well under way, and the term 'romantic' had been established as 'good'.

[33] *English Prose Style* (New York, 1952), p. 85.
[34] *English Prose Style* (London, 1928), p. 195.
[35] *Collected Essays*, p. 123.

VII

SHELLEY AND THE SURREALISTS

1

Read's program of 'rehabilitation' was promulgated with a good deal of energy, and even a certain amount of sensationalism, in two books published in 1936, *In Defence of Shelley & Other Essays*, and *Surrealism*. The title essay of the former volume, and the Introduction Read contributed to the latter (an anthology of critical writings about surrealism), revealed just how bold the new program was. In an unsettling and disturbing manner, Read began to work out the full implications of his position. The key figure from the romantic tradition, it turned out, was not to be Wordsworth – on whom Read had already published a book[1] – but Shelley. Shelley was a test case. If he, with his preoccupation with the ideal and the infinite, could be rehabilitated, it would seem that anyone could be, for Shelley was the very type of the romantic poet against whom the new poets had revolted. Certainly the abstractness of his imagery was at the farthest possible remove from the kind of concrete and perceptual imagery Read insisted upon. Yet despite the difference in their means, both Read an Shelley, as I pointed out earlier, had the same end in view: to strip the veil of familiarity from the world and penetrate to a realm of absolute truth and beauty. If Read were to manage to rehabilitate Shelley, however, it would obviously have to be on some other basis than that of his poetic method.

The long essay "In Defence of Shelley" was occasioned by Eliot's attack on Shelley three years earlier in his book, *The Use of Poetry and the Use of Criticism*. The essay was a defense of Shelley, but more fundamentally it was a defense of Read's own critical principles against Eliot's disapproval. To Eliot, Read's progress in the

---

[1] *Wordsworth* (London, 1930) – a sympathetic study of the relation of Wordsworth's mind and personality to his art.

late 1920's and early 1930's must have seemed increasingly alarming. In 1926 he had welcomed Read as an ally in his own campaign against a psychologically oriented criticism. Reviewing *Reason and Romanticism* and Ramon Fernandez' *Messages* in the *Criterion*, Eliot had contrasted the positions taken by these two critics:

Mr. Read is interested in St. Thomas Aquinas, because he is interested in metaphysical and logical truth; M. Fernandez is interested in Newman, because he is interested in *personality*. The difference between Read and Fernandez is a difference of focus, a difference of value: M. Fernandez is in a sense with Bergson, with the pragmatists, with those who have reached a certain sophistication about "the nature of truth": for Mr. Read, I imagine, . . . there is only truth and error.[2]

Eliot was not quite sure of Read. He had reservations particularly about his interest in psychoanalysis. Both Read and Fernandez, he thought, "are struggling to find an objective truth; both are encumbered by the wipings of psychology. . . . M. Fernandez is in danger of being an idealist without ideals; Mr. Read of being a realist without real objects."[3] But Eliot considered Read to be, on the whole, an ally.

It was, then, a fine bit of irony that Read, six years later in *Form in Modern Poetry*, should not only publicly break with his "best friends in criticism, such as Mr. Eliot" but should set forth a critical doctrine of 'personality' based largely on none other than the ideas of Fernandez. Eliot was not long in reacting to this development. The next year (1933), in *The Use of Poetry and the Use of Criticism*, he expressly rejected Read's division of tradition into 'true' poetry and 'wit-writing'. "Mr. Read's divisions," he said , "are too clear-cut to leave my mind at ease. He considers that the poetic process of a mind like Dryden's and a mind like Wordsworth's are essentially diverse; and he says roundly of Dryden's art, 'Such art is not poetry.' Now I cannot see why Dryden's and Wordsworth's minds should have worked any more differently from each other than those of any other two poets . . . There must . . . be something in common in the poetic process of all poet's minds."[4] Eliot said that Read "seems to charge himself with the task of casting out devils".[5] As to Read's distinction be-

[2] *Criterion*, IV, 4 (1926), 753.
[3] *Ibid.*, 756.
[4] *The Use of Poetry and the Use of Criticism* (London, 1933), p. 83.
[5] *Ibid.*, p. 84.

tween personality and character, Eliot said flatly, "I refuse to be drawn into any discussion of the definition of 'personality' and 'character' ",[6] and "Mr. Herbert Read ... pursues his speculations to a point to which I would not willingly follow him."[7] The point to which Eliot WAS willing to go – and the conclusion his book reaches – was simply this: poetry has a variety of 'uses', but no real definition.

Poetry begins, I dare say, with a savage beating a drum in a jungle, and it retains that essential of percussion and rhythm; hyperbolically one might say that the poet is *older* than other human beings – but I do not want to be tempted to ending on this sort of flourish. I have insisted rather on the variety of poetry, variety so great that all kinds seem to have nothing in common except the rhythm of verse instead of the rhythm of prose: and that does not tell you much about all poetry. Poetry is of course not to be defined by its uses.[8]

Eliot, that is, was reluctant to inquire too closely into the foundations of poetry, preferring rather to talk about its USES than to try to define and justify it philosophically or scientifically. In this way he was able to maintain, more or less, that poetry, whatever it is, is not a substitute for knowledge, religion, or anything else. Eliot tried to regard poetry as poetry, "and not another thing", while recognizing that since the time of Coleridge such an attitude has been increasingly difficult to maintain. For Read, however, such an attitude was altogether impossible to maintain: poetry, as a cognitive mode distinct from the rational mode, was either knowledge or it was nothing.

Read responded by coming to the defense of Shelley. Eliot had attacked Shelley's IDEAS, and through them, the poetry and the man; Read defended the poetry and the ideas by defending Shelley's PERSONALITY. Thus Read's defense was a practical application of the critical theory he had set forth in *Form in Modern Poetry*. Eliot's contention had been that, while Shelley's poetic gifts "were certainly of the first order", his ideas were so "immature", "puerile", "repellent", and "shabby", that they prevented him from enjoying the poetry. He found it impossible to separate the ideas from the poetry, and he was led to formulate – improving on Coleridge and I. A. Richards – his own doctrine of poetry and belief:

[6] *Ibid.*, p. 35.
[7] *Ibid.*, p. 101.
[8] *Ibid.*, p. 155.

"When the doctrine, theory, belief, or 'view of life' presented in a poem is one which the mind of the reader can accept as coherent, mature, and founded on the facts of experience, it interposes no obstacle to the reader's enjoyment, whether it be one that he accept or deny, approve or deprecate. When it is one which the reader rejects as childish or feeble, it may, for a reader of well-developed mind, set up an almost complete check."[9] Now for Read the whole problem of belief and poetry was beside the point. He said he proposed to show the "irrelevance of that mare's nest of Belief, first introduced into the discussion of poetry by our tortuous logodaedalist, Dr. I. A. Richards."[10] For Read, an appreciation of Shelley's poetry depended not on one's belief in Shelley's ideas, but on establishing a sympathetic understanding of Shelley's personality. Once this was established, the ideas could be seen to be not so 'shabby' after all, and the poetry to be of permanent value. "I believe that the knowledge which comes from a complete understanding of a poet's personality is the best basis for the appreciation of his poetry. For it is not a belief in the ideas or dogmas of a poet that is essential for the reader's poetic 'assent', but rather a sympathy with his personality, and this is the sense in which I wish to amend Mr. Eliot's amendment of Dr. Richard's amendment of Coleridge's original suggestion."[11] Read felt that Eliot's attack on Shelley was an attack on the poetic personality itself. "Mr. Eliot", he said, "bears false witness, not so much against poetry itself, as against the nature of the poet."[12]

Read contended that Shelley belonged to a definite psychological type, and that this determined the nature of his poetry, his ideas, and his conduct. The type was one "whose consciousness is incompletely objectified, which is therefore evidently narcissistic, and unconsciously homosexual. Such unconscious homosexuality gives rise to a psychosis of which Shelley shows all the normal symptoms. It determines a line of moral conduct which Shelley exhibits in his life. It determines a quality of imagery and verbal

---

[9] *Ibid.*, p. 96.

[10] *In Defence of Shelley & Other Essays* (London, 1936), p. 9. "In Defence of Shelley" was reprinted in *The True Voice of Feeling* (London, 1953) with a number of revisions and additions.

[11] *Ibid.*, pp. 39—40.

[12] *Ibid.*, p. 10.

expression which is present in Shelley's verse. It has as its concomitant a unity-complex which leads to the development of
those social ideas of a communist tendency which are characteristic of Shelley's political thought."[13] Read amassed a considerable
amount of evidence in support of this analysis of Shelley, and his
approach produced some interesting insights into Shelley's poetry.
His purpose, however, was really not to explain the poetry. It
was to JUSTIFY it on the basis of Shelley's personality. He said
that he would not condemn Shelley's poetry for "failing to achieve
something which was not in the nature of the poet, but praise
it for expressing, with an unsurpassed perfection, qualities which
belonged to the poet and which are of peculiar value to humanity".[14]
And in this lay the real point of Read's essay. His contention was
that the particular neurotic type to which Shelley belonged was
a valuable type; that, in a larger sense, the poet was inevitably
a neurotic; and that neurosis was actually superior to normality.

This chain of reasoning stemmed from the psychological theory
Read had used in his analysis of Shelley – the 'principle of primary
identification' of the psychoanalyst, Trigant Burrow. According
to this theory, primary identification is with the mother, and
development is a process of objectification by which there is finally
established "that *rapport* between the organism and the external
world, which constitutes individual adaptation".[15] When this
process is imperfectly completed, an individual's consciousness
will be incompletely objectified; he will remain, that is, at a stage
relatively closer to the original state of completely subjective
and unconscious 'primary identification'. Now Burrow's ideas
have been useful to Read – here and elsewhere[16] – because they
have the effect of making consciousness itself the source of human
difficulties. For Burrow, the NATURAL state is the preconscious
state; consciousness comes as an interruption, setting up a subject-
object relationship where there had been a continuum. Read
quoted him here as saying, "*Nature abhors consciousness*".[17] All
of this served to confirm Read's notion of poetry as a pre-logical,
pre-grammatical, pre-conceptual kind of cognition, and the poet

[13] *Ibid.*, p. 54.
[14] *Ibid.*, pp. 26—27.
[15] *Ibid.*, p. 43 (quoting Burrow).
[16] See especially *Education through Art* (New York, 1945).
[17] *In Defence of Shelley & Other Essays*, p. 43.

as a man able to recover this primary and elemental state of mind. If, from the standpoint of 'normality' this state of mind was neurotic, then for Read neurosis was really health. He said:

Against this massive self-deception [normality], the neurotic is doomed to protest. It may be that in the process of his individual adaptation to life, his growth has been arrested; he has not, that is to say, completely dissociated himself from his original organic unity with his mother. He has not been fully weaned, he has not been completely *won* for society. Forcibly divorced from his mother, all the strength of his feeling has been transferred to the object of his mother's greatest regard— to himself. Social adaptation consists precisely in getting rid of this self-interest, this autosexuality; in sublimating it, as we say. But such adaptation is really a pretense; under the cover of our conventions we remain disparate, dissociated, resisting the organic wholeness of life. Only the neurotic refuses the compromise. Disparate as he may seem from the point of view of the normality we have achieved, actually he is nearer the source of life, the organic reality; his separateness is really an integrity of personality, an agreement of all the instinctive and affective life of the individual with the organic processes of life in general (the natural unity of our organic life). "If the neurotic regarded individually, or as the embodiment within himself of a societal lesion", writes Dr. Burrow, "is an expression of separatism and patho-logy, the neurotic viewed organically, or as the embodiment within himself of the societal continuum, is no less an expression of confluence and health. If, in the first instance, he is himself the disorder that is his own separatism and unconsciousness, in the second he is the inte-gration that is his own confluence and consciousness".[18]

And the type of the neurotic, Read said, is the type of the artist. "The artist", he quoted Burrow, "feels within . . . the public mind the common soul that underlies it, and senses within it the pain of denied needs identical with his own. This is the unfailing intuition of the artist."[19] Read felt that his distinction between- 'character' and 'personality' had been confirmed here by the author-ity of science. "When I wrote that essay [*Form in Modern Poetry*] I had not read any of Dr. Burrow's works; I was elaborating cer-tain statements of Keats's, and in so far as I was going beyond my own experience, I was relying on my understanding of Freud. I feel now that the truth I was attempting to formulate is amply confirmed by Dr. Burrow (who was trained in the Freudian school) and given a more scientific basis. Literary critics like Mr. Eliot

[18] *Ibid.*, pp. 56—57.
[19] *Ibid.*, pp. 58—59.

may refuse to be drawn into this discussion, but it should now be obvious that such an attitude is merely an avoidance of the essential issue for modern criticism."[20]

"The essential issue for modern criticism". This was for Read, as it had always been, to justify poetry as a mode of apprehension more primary than the rational mode. And he saw Eliot's refusal to discuss the question of personality and character as an avoidance of this issue. Read had met the issue head-on, but his conclusions had driven him to a point where Eliot was not the only critic who "would not willingly follow him". Read had isolated himself from the mainstream of contemporary criticism. For however widespread might be the assumption that poetry represents a primary kind of knowledge, and even that the poet is necessarily a neurotic in relation to society, the dominant approach in contemporary criticism has been altogether different from Read's. It has been to view the poem as a self-contained linguistic structure, to analyze it as a closed system of internal references, and to attempt to do this quite without reference to the personality of the poet. The assumption has been that the poem is deliberately contrived with the full resources of the poet's technique, and that the way into the poem is through a meticulous analysis of the effects wrought by that technique. Consequently the poem, while representing a unique kind of knowledge different from that of 'science', is the product of a technique as rigorous as that of science itself. This view has developed from the basic symbolist notion of the poem as an irrational object rationally constructed. Read could agree that the poem was a form of symbolic discourse, like myth and religion, but he could not agree that it was rationally constructed. His radical (but, after all, logical and consistent) separation of the poetic and the rational modes of cognition had forced him to conceive the entire poetic process as proceeding on a level below consciousness. The way into the poem, therefore, was not by analyzing its technique but simply by submitting oneself to it, and the only judgment to be made was in respect to its authenticity, its 'sincerity'. Fundamentally, of course, the decision involved the question of whether a 'character' or a 'personality' had expressed itself, and on this basis, after showing that Shelley was a type of the poetic personality itself, Read could only conclude that his

[20] *Ibid.*, p. 59.

poetry was of permanent value. Thus the first consequence of the position Read had taken in *Form in Modern Poetry* was to make criticism, in the sense of analysis and judgment, virtually impossible. Its place was taken by sympathy. The critic's primary task was to reach a sympathetic understanding of a poet's personality. If analysis and judgment then followed such an understanding, they did so only as distinctly subsidiary activities.

2

Whether Read's essay did anything to revive a taste for Shelley's poetry may certainly be doubted. (For that revival we are still waiting.) But such was not really his aim. It is open to question, I think, whether he even cared much for Shelley's poetry, as poetry. What he did care for was Shelley's immense claim for the poet as truth-seeker and law-giver. This claim meant everything to Read, and it was this that Eliot, with his attack on Shelley's 'puerile' and 'shabby' ideas, had called into question. Read had to defend Shelley on this point at all costs, and to do so not on the basis of a transcendental philosophy which he felt had been generally discredited, but on grounds that would command some credibility in a scientific age. Thus Shelley's claim was justified on the basis of his super-normal neuroticism – his access, that is, to a superior knowledge, a superior reality closed to normal consciousness. It was the same justification that the surrealists offered for their work, and Read's defense of these twentieth-century artists and poets in his Introduction to the volume *Surrealism* was made on the same grounds as his defense of the nineteenth-century romanticist, Shelley.

That Read should embrace surrealism was only to be expected, for in this development he saw proof of what before had only been a possibility: a pure art of the unconscious, wholly uncontaminated by the rational mode. In his Introduction he contended that surrealism is "a reaffirmation of the romantic principle". Romanticism was reaffirmed here, however, only at the total expense of classicism. "So long", Read said, "as romanticism and classicism were considered as alternative attitudes, rival camps, professions of *faith*, an interminable struggle was in prospect, with the critics as profiteers. But what in effect surrealism claims to do is to resolve the conflict – not, as I formerly hoped, by establishing a synthesis wich I was prepared to call 'reason' or 'humanism' — but by liquidating classicism, by showing its complete irrelevance, its *anaesthetic* effect, its contradiction of the creative impulse."[21] Read was no longer willing to identify the concepts 'classical' and 'romantic' with a historical alternation between two kinds of art, as he had done in *Form in Modern Poetry*. He was no longer willing to allow classicism its own, if inferior, art. The two concepts are in no sense a dialectical contradiction, he now said.

They correspond rather to the husk and the seed, the shell and the kernel. There is a principle of life, of creation, of liberation, and that is the romantic spirit; there is a principle of order, of control, and of repression, and that is the classical spirit . . .. To identify romanticism with revolt . . . is true enough as an historical generalization; but it merely distorts the values involved if such revolt is conceived in purely literary or academic terms. It would be much nearer the truth to identify romanticism with the artist and classicism with society; classicism being the political concept of art to which the artist is expected to conform.[22]

The effect of this distinction was to remove classicism – as anti-art – from any consideration at all. And in similar fashion he settled the introvert-extravert question: "What is questionable is the very existence of such a type as an extravert *artist*. To the degree in which he becomes extravert the artist, we would say, ceases to be, in any essential sense of the word, an artist."[23] This conclusion had been implicit ever since Read separated 'creative' from 'constructive' expression, and 'personality' from 'character', but he had never until now fully carried it out. If a pure art of the unconscious WAS possible, however, there was no longer any need to temporize with the elements of a rational art. Read saw now that the artist stands on one side and society on the other, the artist offering to society the permanent and universal truths which he has tapped within his own self:

What he offers to society is not a bagful of his own tricks, his idiosyncracies, but rather some knowledge of the secrets to which he has had access, the secrets of the self which are buried in every man alike, but which only the sensibility of the artist can reveal to us in all their actuality. This "self" is not the personal possession we imagine it to be; it is largely made up of elements from the unconscious, and the more we learn about the unconscious, the more collective it appears to be –

[21] Introduction to *Surrealism* (London, 1936), pp. 22—23.
[22] *Ibid.*, pp. 26—27.
[23] *Ibid.*, pp. 28—29.

in fact, "a body of common sentiments and thoughts ... universal truths", such as [Sir Herbert] Grierson assumes to be the exclusive concern of the classical artist. But whereas the universal truths of classicism may be merely the temporal prejudices of an epoch, the universal truths of romanticism are coeval with the evolving consciousness of mankind.[24]

The true dialectical opposition, Read held, is between inner and outer reality. The work of art comes as a synthesis in a dialectical contradiction

between the world of objective fact – the sensational and social world of active and economic existence – and the world of subjective fantasy. This opposition creates a state of disquietude, a lack of spiritual equilibrium, which it is the business of the artist to resolve. He resolves the contradiction by creating a synthesis, a work of art which combines elements from both these worlds, eliminates others, but which for the moment gives us a qualitatively new experience – an experience on which we can dwell with equanimity.[25]

Where earlier, as we have seen, he had used psychoanalysis to explain this notion of art as a bridge between subject and object, here he sought a philosophical basis for it. He went to Hegel for a dialectical interpretation of art, but to a Hegel purged of idealism. As Marx had done, Read took the dialectic and discarded the 'Idea', but Read proceeded also to improve on Marx:

As Marx observed in his Preface to the first edition of *Kapital*:
"My dialectic method is not only different from the Hegelian, but its direct opposite. To Hegel, the life-process of the human brain, *i.e.*, the process of thinking, which, under the name of 'the Idea', he even transforms into an independent subject, is the demiurgos of the real world, and the real world is only the external, phenomenal form of 'the Idea'. With me, on the contrary, the ideal is nothing else than the material world reflected by the human mind, and translated into forms of thought".
With the surrealists, we might also say, the ideal is nothing else than the material world reflected by the human mind, and translated into images. But "reflection" and "translation" are not, for us today, such simple mechanical processes as perhaps Marx implies. For us the process is infinitely complicated: a passage through a series of distorting mirrors and underground labyrinths.[26]

Now, if the Marxian 'reflection' and 'translation' were 'simple mechanical processes', they were nonetheless fairly exact processes:

[24] *Ibid.*, p. 27.
[25] *Ibid.*, pp. 40–41.
[26] *Ibid.*, pp. 41–42.

from them came a true reflection and an accurate translation of a real external world. For Read, however, what is known is only the 'image' which appears in the 'distorting mirrors' and emerges from the 'underground labyrinths'. Thus the artist's creation of the image is actually a creation of reality – a 'miracle', as Read has elsewhere called it. Idealism has, in fact, only gone underground in Read's theory: the 'Idea' has been replaced by the 'Image'.

The Introduction to *Surrealism* is an excited and intemperate statement of Read's position. He has since reprinted it under the title, "Surrealism and the Romantic Principle", in *The Philosophy of Modern Art* with this cautionary note:

I am fully conscious of the inadvisability of republishing this polemical essay in a volume which otherwise has some pretension to scientific objectivity. I do so because I feel it would be dishonest to disguise the fact that I am sometimes led away (I do not say led astray) by my sympathies. Those sympathies proceed from my "cult of sincerity" as a poet; and no doubt this is not the only occasion (even in this volume) when the critic abdicates and the poet takes over.[27]

Yet there is really nothing in the essay, other than the general intemperance of the language, for Read to regret, and nothing that could be considered unexpected. He made it clear that he was embracing surrealism not to the exclusion of all other developments in the arts, but as an experiment which had proven the case for a pure art of the unconscious. As such, it had clarified things by showing the direction in which true art always pointed. He quoted André Breton as saying, "Verbal and graphic automatism only represents a *limit* towards which the poet or artist should tend." And Read went on to say, "The opposed limit is represented by all those 'arts of poetry', those academic discourses on painting, in which various ages have sought to codify for all time the laws of art. Between these limits we find the whole range of aesthetic expression, but it is towards the limit of automatism, and away

---

[27] *The Philosophy of Modern Art* (New York, 1953), p. 105. There are minor changes in this version, including a striking 'silent' revision. In the 1936 version (p. 60), one sentence reads: "Surrealism, like Communism, does not call upon artists to surrender their individuality ...". In the 1953 version (p. 127), the same sentence reads: "Surrealism does not, like Communism, call upon artists to surrender their individuality ...". Read's disillusionment with the Communists because of their policies toward artists followed shortly after his Introduction to *Surrealism* was published.

from the limit of rational control that we find the most enduring vitality . . ."[28]. The effect of surrealism, Read maintained, was to make necessary a "revaluation of all aesthetic values", in which the conventional judgments of the academies would be overthrown and we would dare "to travel without a guide, to trust our eyes and ears and our contemporary sensibility . . ."[29]. The consequence, he thought, would be a "rehabilitation of romanticism".

With his own eyes and ears thus opened, and equipped, so to speak, with a measure which had 'automatism' at one end and 'rational control' at the other, Read looked at the tradition of English literature and pointed out some areas in which he thought a revaluation should take place. For one thing, the 'supreme poetic quality' of the ballads must be recognized. They are, he said, "the most fundamental and authentic type of all poetry . . . to some degree automatic, and illustrate the intrinsic nature of surrealist poetry".[30] For another, the 'inescapable significance' of Shakespeare must be acknowledged. Read claimed the "rehabilitation of Shakespeare's genius" as "the work of specifically romantic critics, beginning with Coleridge and ending, for the moment, with Middleton Murry".[31] Read's attitude to Shakespeare here, and elsewhere, was one of unashamed idolatry. Shakespeare is always available to him for a kind of ultimate appeal. "Almost daily", he had said in *Form in Modern Poetry*, "I lift my voice in thanksgiving for this immortal witness: a poet who was no pedant nor moralist, a man of no character nor convictions, of no caste nor culture, but just a naked sensibility living in its own gusto, reaching after nothing more distant than the impassioned accents of its own voice as it issued from the 'terrible crystal' of an intuitive mind."[32] In Shakespeare the skilled workman, the conscious craftsman, Read had apparently no interest at all. Still another area for revaluation was that earlier interest of his, metaphysical poetry. The relations between metaphysics and poetry, Read thought, could bear psychological examination. "From our present point of view", he said, "it is only necessary to affirm and prove that even in its most intellectual forms poetry acquires its poetic

[28] Introduction to *Surrealism*, p. 29.
[29] *Ibid.*, p. 45.
[30] *Ibid.*, p. 46.
[31] *Ibid.*, p. 47.
[32] *Form in Modern Poetry*, p. 73.

quality by a process which brings it into line with the irrational sources of lyrical and romantic poetry."[33] Thus even when most 'intellectual', true poetry, for Read, approaches the limit of 'automatism' rather than 'rational control'. And finally, Read thought that a revaluation should lead to a lifting of the 'moral ban' against such poets as Shelley, Byron, and Swinburne, who "are judged by standards which must be repudiated".

If, like Mr. Eliot, we believe that "literary criticism should be completed by criticism from a definite ethical and theological standpoint", then a revaluation becomes all the more necessary. For the ethical and theological standpoint from which we should then judge Shelley would be much nearer to Shelley's ethics and theology than to the ethics and theology of the Church. And the moral shudder that the very name of Byron sends through our bourgeois homes would be intensified by our acclamation. Byron is not, in any obvious degree, a superrealist poet; but he is a superrealist personality. He is the only English poet who might conceivably occupy, in our hierarchy, the position held in France by the Marquis de Sade. The function of such figures is to be so positive in their immorality, that morality becomes negative by comparison. They show, by the more-than-human energy of their evil, that evil too, as Milton was compelled to admit, has its divinity. In short, they reveal the conventionality of all systems of morality.[34]

What Read apparently meant here was that if criticism must have an ultimate ethical and theological basis, then we must find this basis not in a revealed religion or an ethical system, but in those 'superrealist' personalities who have perceived the sham of normality and convention. This seems quite the opposite of Eliot's contention, although it was logical enough from Read's standpoint. The ultimate justification for surrealism, and thus for poetry itself, was for Read precisely ethical and moral – but in reference to a super-ethics, a super-morality.

Surrealism, then, really implied for Read a revaluation of values, not just aesthetic values. His romantic principle, which he believed surrealism had reaffirmed, was "a principle of life, of creation, of liberation". It could not be confined to the field of aesthetics. To 'rehabilitate' romanticism, on Read's terms, was to rehabilitate not a literary tradition but life itself. He came, like Shelley, as a prophet and law-giver, calling on men to heed the god within them, and to honor the poets who speak with the divine voice.

[33] Introduction to *Surrealism*, p. 50.
[34] *Ibid.*, p. 52.

VIII

PSYCHOANALYSIS AND ORGANIC FORM

1

By the mid-1930's Read had become contemporary criticism's most articulate and persuasive spokesman for the doctrine of poetic inspiration, a doctrine at least as old as Plato and throughout the history of criticism always current in some form or other. It was Read's task to take this ancient notion of the inspired and holy poet and restate it in contemporary terms: to offer a theoretical rationale for poetic inspiration which might be credited in a scientific age. For this rationale he turned to psychoanalysis. He turned to it now, as he had before, solely in the interest of poetry. Where the psychoanalysts aimed to help the neurotic attain some understanding and thus some control over the irrational forces within him, Read, speaking for the poet, aimed to unleash those forces. Like an ancient poet he invoked the Muse, but he called her the Id.

In 1937, in *Art and Society*, Read made a fairly systematic attempt to state the doctrine of poetic inspiration in terms of Freud's theory of the mind. He adapted here to his own purpose Freud's revision of his earlier theories, particularly the three-fold division of the mind he had proposed in his *New Introductory Lectures*. The work of art, Read said, has correspondences with each of Freud's mental divisions – Id, Ego, and Super-ego.

It derives its energy, its irrationality and its mysterious power from the id, which is to be regarded as the source of what we usually call inspiration. It is given formal synthesis and unity by the ego; and finally it may be assimilated to those ideologies or spiritual aspirations which are the peculiar creation of the super-ego.[1]

This explains, he said, the aesthetic unity that underlies the most diverse objects of art, for they have their origin in the 'impersonal

[1] *Art and Society* (New York, 1937), p. 201.

and unchanging' experiences of the id, go through a process of 'elaboration and sublimation', and are finally "clothed in the ideologies of the super-ego".

The ego intermediates between the primal forces and the ultimate ideal; it gives form and physical harmony to what issues forceful but amorphous and perhaps terrifying from the id; and then, in the super-ego, it gives to these forms and harmonies the ideological tendencies and aspirations of religion, morality, and social idealism.[2]

Upon Freud's three-fold division, however, Read proceeded to superimpose his own two-fold division. He separated the super-ego from the ego and id, just as he had separated 'character' from 'personality'. The 'essential function' of the artist, he said, is fulfilled by the ego and id alone. From the 'seething cauldron' of the id, the artist "snatches some archetypal form, some instinctive association of words, images, or sounds, which constitute the basis of the work of art".[3] The artist's 'primary function' is this "capacity to materialize the instinctual life of the deepest levels of the mind", and it is because he draws from the collective unconscious that his work has such strange power over us. But the archetypal fantasms are too raw, too shocking, and "the artist must exercise a certain skill lest the bare truth repel us. He therefore invests his creation with superficial charms; wholeness or perfection, a due proportion or harmony, and clarity; and these are the work of his conscious mind, his ego. There, I think, the essential function of art ends . . ."[4] Society, however, makes the artist an exponent of the "moral and ideal emanations of the super-ego, and art thus becomes the hand-maid of religion or morality or social ideology". Art thereby suffers, Read said, for the message becomes more important than the 'mode of conveyance", and it is the mode which matters.

But by the mode we mean more than the externals of beauty; we mean above all the driving energy, the uprush of forces from the well of the unconscious.

Ideas, and all the rational superstructure of the mind, can be conveyed by the instruments of thought or science; but those deeper intuitions of the mind, which are neither rational nor economic, but which

[2] Ibid.
[3] Ibid., p. 203.
[4] Ibid., pp. 203—204.

nevertheless exercise a changeless and eternal influence on successive generations of men – these are accessible only to the mystic and the artist, and only the artist can give them material representation.[5]

Now nothing of this account of the artistic process is to be found in Freud, and it is significant that it entails a complete reversal of Freud's reality-principle. Read was generalizing from a 'casual suggestion' he said Freud had made "that certain practices of mystics may succeed in upsetting the normal relations between the different regions of the mind, so that, for example, the perceptual system becomes able to grasp relations in the deeper layers of the ego and in the id which would otherwise be inaccessible to it"[6]. The artist's practice, Read thought, is identical to this, and the consequence is that the artist overturns the reality-principle. Freud, Read said, had pictured the ego as that part of the id which is in contact with the external world and which must present a true picture of that world: "By means of the reality-test it has to eliminate any element in this picture of the external world which is a contribution from internal sources of excitation . . . It interpolates between desire and action the procrastinating factor of thought . . . In this way it dethrones the pleasure-principle . . . and substitutes for it the reality-principle . . ."[7] Read believed that the artist exactly reverses this procedure:

All this is true of the formation of the normal individual, but in the case of the artist there is an exception; *he* does not eliminate any element which is a contribution from internal sources of excitation; *his* purpose is precisely to introduce such elements, and so disturb the even and orderly surface of the ordinary man's conception of reality by the introduction of forces from that deeper level of being which we call the id. It is *his* desire to evade the procrastinating factor of thought and give to the world all the immediacy and vitality of his intuitions, his perceptions of the instinctual processes of his mind.[8]

On this basis, there would seem to be no way to distinguish between art and insanity. Where for Freud art was always a way back to reality, for Read it WAS reality. Freud thought that the artist differed from other neurotics in being able to objectify his

[5] *Ibid.*, p. 204.
[6] *Ibid.*, p. 202 (quoting from Freud).
[7] *Ibid.*, p. 227 (quoting again from Freud).
[8] *Ibid.*, p. 228.

fantasies and make them attractive to others. The artist, in other words, looks at his objectivized fantasy and knows it for what it is; and because others take pleasure in it, he finds, Freud said, "he has won – through his phantasy – what before he could only win in phantasy: honour, power, and the love of women".[9] In his *New Introductory Lectures*, Freud remarked, "Art is almost always harmless and beneficent, it does not seek to be anything else but an illusion. Save in the case of a few people who are, one might say, obsessed by art, it never dares to make any attacks on the realm of reality."[10] Although the *New Introductory Lectures* were Read's principal source for his discussion in *Art and Society*, he did not quote this passage. And indeed, Freud would surely have considered Read to be "obsessed by art". For Read thought the artist has access to a reality so superior – in fact, so startling – that he must disguise it from the public. The raw images of the id, Read said, would be "too much for us; such art we should describe as uncanny, *unheimlich*". The artist therefore renders his images palatable by giving them the charm and pleasure of form; he "tames" them, much as the dream censor conceals the latent content of the dream. His "care must be to compromise; so to control the outflow of his instinctive energies that they do not unduly alarm or antagonize the normal individual. He does this by disguising his lawless images – by giving them a clothing of symbol and myth which makes them acceptable to the public at large."[11] From the standpoint of the philosophical position Freud set forth in the *New Introductory Lectures* – the nineteenth-century scientific *Weltanschauung* which is firmly anchored in an external world of real objects[12] – Read would surely appear as a man who 'dares' to attack the 'realm of reality'. Read's conception of reality was fundamentally incompatible with Freud's, and to make use of Freud's psychoanalytical theories, Read had, in effect, removed them from the philosophical assumptions in which they were set.

[9] Sigmund Freud, A *General Introduction to Psychoanalysis* (New York, 1953), pp. 385—386. Read, who has often quoted this sentence of Freud's, has never been satisfied with this view of the artist.

[10] Sigmund Freud, *New Introductory Lectures on Psychoanalysis* (London, 1933), p. 205.

[11] *Art and Society*, p. 228.

[12] See Chapter XXXV, "A Philosophy of Life".

Read had again exploited psychoanalysis for his own ends. He had taken from Freud only what he needed – support for his view of art as a primary kind of knowledge and of the artistic process as essentially an immediate act. The 'reality–test', with its "procrastinating factor of thought", is for Read the rational mode of cognition. The artist 'evades' this through a mystical, non-temporal act, and presents his intuitions in all their 'immediacy and vitality'. Moreover, since art had always appealed to Read as a contradiction to the flow of time and the flux of existence, Freud's notion of the anti-temporal nature of the id was particularly impressive. Freud's view, he said, was that "in the id there is nothing corresponding to the idea of time, no recognition of the passage of time, and . . . no alteration of mental processes by the passage of time". The contents of the id therefore have that permanence and universality, that contradiction of time, which for Read is characteristic of art. "If we consider", Read said, "that this region, this cauldron, into which the artist is able to peer is a region of timeless entities, then we seem to have some explanation of the source of the vital energy which is transmitted to the artist's creative impulse, and at least a suggestion of an explanation of the universal appeal of what the artist is inspired to express. For what is timeless is by the same token universal."[13]

That there was more of Read than of Freud in this view of the artistic process was only to be expected, since the assumptions and aims of the two men were so different. But Read believed he had as much right to draw his evidence from psychology as the psychologists have to draw theirs from art.[14] Actually, there is more support in Jung's work for the notion of the poet as an inspired medium than in Freud's, and it was to Jung that Read increasingly turned in the years ahead.[15] Read tried to restate the ancient doctrine of poetic inspiration in contemporary terms, and with all his faults he remained our most notable exponent of it. That this doctrine should be advocated in a scientific age so seriously, so earnestly, and with as much show of intellectual support as Read has been able to muster, is enough to give one

[13] Art and Society, p. 225.
[14] See Introduction to Collected Essays.
[15] See, e.g., "The Dynamics of Art", Eranos Jahrbuch 1952, XXI (Zurich, 1953), reprinted in The Forms of Things Unknown (London, 1960).

pause. The point to be borne in mind, I think, is that Read's
view of poetry as knowledge, different in kind from prosaic, or scientific, knowledge, is a common contemporary assumption. But
Read, unlike those critics who approach the poem through an
analysis of its technique, has never been able to see how, if poetry
is a unique kind of knowledge, the poet can write the poem with
the prosaic, or scientific, part of his mind. He must, rather, be a
vessel or medium for forces more powerful than he. From the
beginning, therefore, Read has persisted in his conviction that the
essentially poetic part of the poem is 'given', and that the poet's
exercise of technique and the critic's analysis of it are distinctly
subsidiary activities.

Not that Read ever finally solved the problem of form involved
in his view. He only managed to pursue it as far as possible while
still remaining consistent with his assumptions. In *Art and Society*,
where his subject was primarily the plastic arts, he again had
trouble in getting from the 'given' image to the actual work of
art. By superimposing his own two-fold division of mental life on
Freud's three-fold division, Read had altogether removed from
consideration the 'message', which is dictated by the super-ego
and is a 'perversion' of art. This left him only the 'mode of conveyance', which comprised the two processes, 'inspiration' and
'elaboration'. 'Inspiration' referred to the raw images which issue
from the id, and 'elaboration' to the 'superficial charms' of form
with which the conscious ego invests these images. The result
was a curious variation of the 'sugar-coating' theory of form. Where
this theory has traditionally meant that a content of rational
truth or conventional morality is enclosed in a pleasurable form,
in Read's theory the instinctual images which might otherwise
be terrifying to the 'normal' public were so inclosed. Since rational
truth and conventional morality had been removed to another
plane, they had no bearing on the matter at all. Read's values
were all the other way around. He had claimed in the Introduction
to *Surrealism* that the 'universal truths' contained in the collective
unconscious took the place for the romantic artist of that "body
of common sentiments and thoughts" which had been the concern
of the classical artist. And so, in much the same manner that the
Renaissance classicists – for whom Read has never had any use –
thought the delights of art should be used to sweeten instruction,
Read believed his romantic artist should add consciously a "whole-

ness or perfection, a due proportion or harmony, and clarity",
as a palliative necessitated by the 'normal' audience.[16]

2

In Read's poetic theory, his conclusions were exactly the same,
but because of the difference in medium they seemed even more
paradoxical. There had, for example, always been a difficulty in
his view of metaphor as an equivalent for the highest poetic visions.
Did not metaphor inevitably carry with it a taint of 'art'? He
decided now that it usually did. His interest in surrealism induced
him to attempt the writing of dream-poems – to try to translate,
that is, a dream directly into poetry, with no conscious mediation
or deliberation. The resulting poems, he believed, were as close to
being automatic as he could come. But when he studied them he
discovered that the metaphors and similes they contained were
mostly additions by his conscious mind. The 'pure' part of the
poem was the direct expression of the visual dream-image.

In his Introduction to *Surrealism* Read printed one of these
dream poems and distinguished what in it was genuinely given
to him from the dream and what was added in the process of writing. One metaphor (actually a simile) he said was genuine: "I lift
my hands and make a pass/ which casts upon the facing wall/
a silhouette hovering like a baffled bird." Another was false:
" . . . our racing shadows rise and fall / like waves against the
bleached cliff". Now to the reader there is no way to distinguish
between these, but to Read there was, because he had SEEN the
one and had THOUGHT OF the other: " . . . the image of the baffled
bird – the fluttering shadow like a bird beating against a win-
dowpane – *occurred to me in my dream*. In this it differs from the
wave-image I have used to describe the shadows of our bodies on
the walls of the labyrinth, which is a conscious image produced
in the process of writing the poem."[17] Read went on to say that
he would "on that account call it a metaphor rather than an image".
He was beginning here to clarify something that had long been

---

[16] Herbert J. Muller, in *Science and Criticism* (New Haven, 1943), noted
this sugar-coating conception of form as "an odd corollary of Read's thesis".
But it is not so odd, if we remember the complete reversal of values which
Read's thesis entails.

[17] Introduction to *Surrealism*, p. 73.

unclear in his theory. He had used the term 'image' loosely to mean either a sensory impression (usually visual) or a figure of speech; but he had never explained how the genuine poetic figure was to be distinguished from the false 'wit-writing' figure. What he was saying now was that the comparison involved in a figure had itself to come from the unconscious to be genuine: the baffled bird, that is, was seen in his dream in the shadow cast by the hands. The comparison, therefore, was integral, indissoluble – not fundamentally a matter of words at all but of VISION.[18] The genuine figure, in other words, was quite literally an 'image'. Once the vision was recorded, however, the final step in writing the poem was exactly the same as the process of 'elaboration' Read distinguished in respect to the plastic arts: "Then, to disguise any gaps or incoherency, the conscious mind of the poet has worked over the poem, and given it that smooth facade which is generally demanded by the literary conventions of an age, and which in any case makes for ease of communication."[19]

The difference between the 'image' and the 'metaphor', then, was the difference between a comparison or relation 'seen' or 'given' and one searched for. Read would not avoid figures, he said, or even rhymes, if they 'came' to him. He did not claim that all poems should be records of dreams, but he did think that the dream-poem proved the true origin of the image. "It is not every poem that has the integral character of a dream", he said, "but every authentic image is conceived in the unconscious."[20]

In his theory, Read was getting farther and farther away from the poem, as poem. Even his notion of an 'equivalence' between 'thought' and 'word', between image and expression, was no longer so clear here as it had been. For if we push far enough along this line of reasoning, the 'word' side of the equation tends to dissolve and we have left only the pure dream-image – the 'real' poem. Why, after all, write the actual poem? Read's general answer to this objection was, I think, that the poem must be written because it serves as a bridge between inner and outer reality, a neces-

---

[18] In making his distinction between 'image' and 'metaphor', Read used here (and also in his essay, "Obscurity in Poetry") a similar distinction made by the French critic, Pierre Reverdy.

[19] Introduction to *Surrealism*, p. 76.

[20] *Ibid.*, p. 77.

sary synthesis in the dialectical contradiction between them. Yet if this be the case, one would think he would have wanted to engage the whole mind in effecting such a synthesis, and in particular the conscious part of the mind which is in contact with outer reality. But this would have meant that he would be including the rational, discursive mode which he had given over to 'science', and this he could not do.

The result was more of the same inconclusive struggle to account for the poem that we have seen before. In "Obscurity in Poetry", an essay published in 1936 in the same volume with "In Defense of Shelley", Read argued that there is a positive value in obscurity. From his premises, this is of course an inescapable conclusion. Using Vico's notion of 'poetic metaphysics' and a 'poetic logic' existing prior to prose reasoning, and Bergson's notion of a poetic or mystical projection beyond the concepts and words of normal thought processes,[21] he contended that the poet must be obscure to be clear. Only, in other words, by wholly abandoning prose logic could he be understood at all. This essay may, like "In Defense of Shelley", have been prompted by some remarks of Eliot's in *The Use of Poetry and the Use of Criticism*. Eliot had claimed that there is no particular virtue in obscurity as such, and had said that he believed "the poet naturally prefers to write for as large and miscellaneous an audience as possible".[22] Eliot was quite willing to put 'meaning' into the poem to satisfy the reader's expectations "while the poem does its work upon him: much as the imaginary burglar is always provided with a bit of nice meat for the house-dog".[23] In this, and in his statement that the "ideal medium for poetry . . . is the theatre",[24] it was evident that Eliot (whatever his poetic practice) was careful not to theorize himself away from the poem and the audience. For Read, however, whose theory encompassed 'poetry' but not the poem or the reader, such an attitude must have appeared as the most dangerous kind of temporizing.

Read's final attempt during the 1930's (and I do not think he ever went beyond it) to get theoretically from the image to the

---

[21] Read's anti-Bergsonism had long since disappeared.
[22] *The Use of Poetry and the Use of Criticism*, p. 152.
[23] *Ibid.*, p. 151.
[24] *Ibid.*, p. 153.

poem, occurred in the essay, "Myth, Dream, and Poem".[25] Here
he started from the premise that the myth is the dream of the
race, and that the individual touches this mythical mind in his
dreams. "This mythical mind is the mind we all know in our dreams,
partially, incoherently, but the poet knows it with a penetrating
and selective validity."[26] But where the myth "persists by virtue
of its imagery" and is thus translatable from one language to
another, the poem consists of imagery allied to an 'essence' of
language and is thus untranslatable. The problem was to account
for this 'essence', these 'precise verbal equivalents'. To do so by
reference to the conscious mind would be to destroy the poem's
bond with the dream and the myth. "There is not . . . any clear
distinction", he said, "between the dream and the work
of art, for . . . the works of art which survive are those
which most nearly approach to the illogical order of the dream.
Art retreats before the intellect, or grows stiff and atrophied and
survives only in the records of academies."[27] Accordingly, Read
explained the poem's language as a direct 'precipitation' in a dream-
like or trance-like state. He said the myth's "vivid eidetic energy
acts like a catalyst among the suspended verbal molecules and pre-
cipitates just those which clothe the image in the brightest sheath
of words".[28] The poetic process takes place entirely in the unconscious mind, and is governed by what he called a 'law of attraction'
which selects equivalents in visual image, verbal expression,
musical expression, temporal extension. There is the image like a
photograph film and there is at the same time an automatically
selected and adjusted sound-track, perfectly expressing and fault-
lessly accompanying the imagery."[29]

Thus behind everything is an 'eidetic energy' which 'precipi-
tates' words, rhythm, and duration or length – all without conscious
deliberation. But the result of this process is not, except possibly
in the case of *Kubla Khan* and a few other works, a poem; and
although Read included two more of his own dream-poems in the

[25] Published in *transition*, no. 27 (1938), and reprinted the same year
in *Collected Essays*.

[26] "Myth, Dream, and Poem", *Collected Essays*, p. 103.

[27] *Ibid.*, p. 104.

[28] *Ibid.*, pp. 104—105.

[29] *Ibid.*, pp. 109—110.

essay and called on modern poets "to test the theory by rigorous experiment", he still had to account for poetry as it actually exists:

What I am saying – the conclusion I am driven to – is that pure poetry is ideal or absolute poetry, and not real or actual poetry; that poetry is an essence which we have to dilute with grosser elements to make it viable or practicable. A poem that is pure imagery would be like a statue of crystal – something too cold and transparent for our animal senses. We therefore cloud the poem with metaphors and similes, which are our personal and human associations; we add to it sentiments and ideas, until finally the essential imagery is completely obscured and we are left with verbal rhetoric.[30]

Here we have the notion of diluting an essence, rather than adding a palliation, as in the plastic arts. But the two notions are really the same: in both cases the raw strength of images from the unconscious is modified. We make the poem humanly approachable by means of metaphors and similes, sentiments and ideas, which satisfy our 'animal senses'. We turn the ideal into the actual – or, in a sense, 'poetry' into a poem.

Where in this conception is the 'organic' principle which Read had set forth in *Form in Modern Poetry?* I noted earlier that he had not been able to make this principle work satisfactorily on anything longer than a very short poem, really a single image emerging from a single creative moment. But it is questionable whether it works even that well here. If form is organic "when a work of art has its own inherent laws, originating with its very invention and fusing in one vital unity both structure and content",[31] then surely this dilution of essence with 'grosser elements' is not organic. Yet it is necessary if we are to get from ideal to actual poetry, from essence to existence. The organic analogy, used normally and appropriately by romantic theorists, is that of the plant or any living thing. The words 'automatism' and 'automatic', however, bring to mind the opposing analogy of the machine, and it is significant that Read described the creative moment in terms of a 'photograph film' and an 'automatically selected and adjusted sound-track'. In a state of complete trance, the poet is only an instrument, an extension of his pencil, and his function is as automatic as that of any machine. Read's view of the poetic process here –

[30] *Ibid.*, p. 110.
[31] *Form in Modern Poetry*, p. 3.

like his view of the creative process in the visual arts – was actually a kind of inverted classicism. In the classical doctrine of 'nature' (genius, inspiration) plus 'art' (judgment, skill), we find the poem adequately accounted for, but we have to accept a view of the poetic process that emphasizes the JUDGMENT involved in achieving a relation of fitness between form and content. In the romantic doctrine, on the other hand, both 'nature' and 'art' are subsumed under the notion of organism, and the relationship between form and content is not so much that existing in a finished artifact as in the growth and development of a living thing. In this view of the poetic process, 'nature' predominates. Coleridge, for example, attacked the notion of Shakespeare as a child of nature, maintaining instead that his judgment was equal to his genius; but the effect of his argument was to make judgment a part of his genius. For Coleridge, Shakespeare was not an example of judgment imposed – or sometimes not imposed – upon genius, as he had been for Dryden and Dr. Johnson, but of judgment and genius as a single force. Thus where Johnson could praise Shakespeare's genius but criticize his judgment, Coleridge could not make this distinction: he could only praise. Read, too, could only praise Shakespeare, but unlike Coleridge, he could not even discuss Shakespeare's judgment. For judgment belongs to 'art' and is thus no essential part of the poetic process. This process belongs altogether to 'nature', consisting as it does in a direct precipitation of words from vision. When the poet then 'dilutes' this precipitation so that ordinary human beings can approach it, he exercises judgment and skill. Thus Read had arrived at something more like the classical notion of a distinction between 'nature' and 'art' than the romantic notion of organism which includes both. What Coleridge had tried to keep together, Read took apart. Read's conception, far from effecting an organic fusion of 'nature' and 'art', makes the poet into, first, an instrument, a mechanism which merely receives what is 'given', and, second, a conscious human being who awakens and exercises his skill in disguising what he has received. To the scornful question Coleridge directed at the child-of-nature advocates, "Does God choose idiots by whom to convey divine truths to man?"[32] Read would have to answer that the poet is really two persons, the most essential of whom is indeed an idiot.

[32] S. T. Coleridge, *Shakespearean Criticism*, Vol. I, p. 202.

ANARCHY AND SUPERREALITY

1

In 1938 Read assembled certain of his critical writings under the title, *Collected Essays in Literary Criticism*, in this way marking off a permanent body of critical work by which he was willing to stand. The essays collected represented more than fifteen years of development, the earliest ("The Nature of Metaphysical Poetry") dating from 1923, and the latest ("Myth, Dream, and Poem") from 1938.[1] Divided into two sections, "General Theories" and "Particular Studies", the book displayed Read's ability both as theoretician and practical critic. The "Particular Studies", ranging in time from Froissart to Henry James, represent a kind of critical work that Read often did exceedingly well: the attempt to discriminate the exact quality of a writer's mind. His method was partly biographical, partly psychological, partly literary or aesthetic. He was probably least successful when he yielded to the temptation to psychoanalyze his subject; yet the analysis was offered, not insisted upon. With taste and sympathy, Read assessed the writers' minds in a way that can be directly useful in understanding their works. His kind of 'genetic' criticism is seen here at its best, I think, and even where the essays now seem dated, they remain still suggestive and helpful. In their psychological orientation

---

[1] With the exception of "Myth, Dream, and Poem", all the essays were reprinted (some with revisions and under different titles) from previous collections. From *Reason and Romanticism* came "The Nature of Metaphysical Poetry", "The Nature of Criticism", "Tobias Smollett", "Charlotte and Emily Bronte", and "Poetic Diction" (in part); from *The Sense of Glory*, "Froissart", "Malory", "Descartes", "Swift", "Vauvenargues", "Sterne", "Hawthorne", "Bagehot", and "Henry James"; from *Form in Modern Poetry*, "Organic and Abstract Form", "The Personality of the Poet", "Poetic Diction" (in part), "The Structure of the Poem", and "The Poetic Experience"; from *In Defence of Shelly & Other Essays*, "Obscurity in Poetry", "Coventry Patmore", and "Gerard Manly Hopkins".

these studies depend on the "General Theories" set forth in the first part of the book, but they are not, like "In Defence of Shelley", demonstrations of the consequences when the theory is carried out to its logical conclusion and sympathy for a writer's personality supersedes judgment of his work. If we were to judge Read's position from these "Particular Studies" (excluding "Descartes", which is more philosophical than literary), we would hardly expect a theory as radical as the one we find in the theoretical section of the same book.

The "General Theories" Read offered in *Collected Essays* represented, in effect, a summation of the critical position he had been exploring during the 1930's. He divided this section into two parts: "The Nature of Poetry", and "The Nature of Criticism". The first of these comprised what had been *Form in Modern Poetry*, now slightly revised, with titles given to its various sections, and expanded by the addition of three essays: "The Nature of Metaphysical Poetry", "Obscurity in Poetry", and "Myth, Dream, and Poem".[2] Where *Form in Modern Poetry* had been an exploratory statement of Read's neo-romantic position, it became when rearranged and expanded in *Collected Essays* an exposition of that position as he had worked it out. And his unresolved difficulties were fully apparent here. Read had based his argument in *Form in Modern Poetry* on the Coleridgean notion of organic form, a notion which in his hands had failed to account adequately for the long poem, and which had become, as we have seen, quite unrecognizable by the time he wrote "Myth, Dream, and Poem" and "Obscurity in Poetry". Yet those two essays were here sandwiched in before the concluding section of what had been *Form in Modern Poetry*, serving, in effect, as part of the argument of that book. And "The Nature of Metaphysical Poetry", although it had nothing to do with the problem of form, became now also part of the same argument. Yet this early essay did not disturb the argument, since it was concerned entirely with the poet's mission as revealer of a unifying knowledge, which, after all, was still Read's chief interest. Indeed, the title, "The Nature of Poetry", which Read gave this part of his theoretical section,

[2] Part of the early essay, "The Future of Poetry", from *Reason and Romanticism*, in which Read had argued for a wholly instinctual basis for the organization of poetic rhythm, was preserved here (pp. 49—56) by splicing it to a section of *Form in Modern Poetry*.

makes sense only if 'poetry' is understood to refer to a cognitive process, rather than to the making of poems. Despite his honesty and earnestness, Read could not solve the formal problem because in the last analysis it was always the 'form' of this process, not the form of a poem, that he was concerned with. The second part of this section, "The Nature of Criticism", dealt wholly with the psychological approach to literature. It consisted of a single essay, a considerably revised version of the early work, "Psycho-analysis and Criticism". In the middle of this Read had now added a long excursus on inspiration, taken intact from *Art and Society*, which, as we saw in the last chapter, identified the artist with the mystic as one who overthrows the reality-principle and short-circuits normal mental processes. For Read, then, the 'nature' of criticism was altogether psychological, a conclusion that certainly followed from his view of the 'nature' of poetry.

Collected Essays in Literary Criticism summed up Read's literary theory, but it was *Poetry and Anarchism*, published also in 1938, which completed the outline of his 'rehabilitation' of romanticism. Read had founded his theory on an absolute separation of the poetic and rational processes; yet the poet is, after all, a man, and if he does not exercise his rational faculties in the process of poetry, he does so in the process of living. It is at this point, therefore, that the poet, for Read, transforms himself into the anarchist. What is in art a romantic principle becomes in life an anarchic principle. The anarchist is the poet, but on the plane of life, not of art. On this plane he employs his conscious, rational mind, discovering the order implicit in the universe and ordering his own life according to this natural law. In doing so, he is, Read said, philosophically a realist:

I have always tended to see in communism a reaffirmation of certain metaphysical doctrines which Europe possessed in the Middle Ages, and then lost in the rising tide of humanism, liberalism, and idealism . . . It is very necessary that we should once again admit the universalism of truth and submit our lives to the rule of reason. This universalism and this reason, as Catholic philosophers insist, are aspects of realism . . . As communists we speak of our dialectical materialism, but we mean our dialectical realism. The negation of the idealism of Hegel is realism: the realism of Aristotle, of Albertus and Aquinas; the realism of the empirical tradition of modern science.

. . . A realistic rationalism . . . establishes a universal order of thought, which is a necessary order of thought because it is not man-imposed, but natural; and each man finding this order finds his freedom.

Modern anarchism is a reaffirmation of this natural freedom, of this direct communion with universal truth. Anarchism rejects the man-made systems of government, which are instruments of individual and class tyranny; it seeks to recover the system of nature, of man living in accordance with the universal truth of reality. It denies the rule of kings and castes, of churches and parliaments, to affirm the rule of reason, which is the rule of God.[3]

In anarchism, then, idealism is negated. For the anarchist the world is a world of real objects in which he discovers that which already exists: the order of the natural law. Transformed in this curious manner into anarchism, that strain in Read's thought now re-emerged which had been so pronounced in the 1920's, when he had appeared as an apostle of reason, calling for a revival of Thomism against the 'subjective trend' in western philosophy. All truths now seemed to him to be derived from the physical world. "Is it not possible", he asked, "that the only truth is the law and structure of the universe, so far as we can observe it and that all other truths are analogies derived from aspects of this physical order? Justice, for example, on this assumption, is an analogy of equal quantities; beauty is an analogy of symmetry and balance; goodness is perfect growth." And our knowledge of these truths, he said, we owe to reason, which is "the faculty by means of which we discover the laws of the universe and attempt to relate them to some general conception of its organization".[4]

This 'realistic rationalism', however, was not the whole story. Read had negated idealism, but not subjectivism. For balanced against the discovery of a world of real objects and its laws is the spontaneous creation in art of a world of the imagination:

It is tempting to identify our aesthetic emotions with our awareness of the structural harmony of the universe, but a closer examination of the aesthetic creations of mankind shows that their forms tend to depart

[3] *Poetry and Anarchism* (London, 1938), pp. 95—96. By "communism" here Read did not refer to the program of the Communist party. This book marked his public disavowal of the Communists because of their repressive measures against Soviet artists and poets, and his adoption of anarchism, a doctrine which the Communists considered utopian and dangerous. Henceforth Read was to be as far outside the mainstream of leftist politics as he already was outside that of contemporary criticism.

[4] *Ibid.*, p. 123.

in some degree from the mathematical patterns which result from physical laws. The emotion we experience when we perceive the form of a crystal or of the solar system is not the same as the emotion we experience when we read Shakespeare's poetry or listen to Beethoven's music. This latter emotion is rather the thrill we experience from daring to depart from the patterns inherent in the universe. Art is thus an adventure into the unknown, and therefore purely subjective. This has not always been perceived, and a confusion has arisen between the imitation of universal patterns (the "beauty" of classical art) and the creation of free patterns (which is art properly so-called).[5]

Thus the critical speculation that for centuries revolved around the general concept, 'imitation', is here dismissed as 'confusion'. Art, for Read, is wholly the creation of a new world, not the imitation of an existing one. It is 'purely subjective': insofar as it departs from a world of real objects, it is art; insofar as it conforms to that world it is not.

'Discovery' and 'creation', Read said, are different processes and must be kept absolutely separate:

We have two possibilities: to discover truth, and to create beauty. We make a profound mistake if we confuse these two activities, attempting to discover beauty and to create truth. If we attempt to create truth, we can only do so by imposing on our fellow men an arbitrary and idealistic system which has no relation to reality; and if we attempt to discover beauty we look for it where it cannot be found – in reason, in logic, in experience. Truth is in reality, in the visible and tangible world of sensation; but beauty is in unreality, in the subtle and unconscious world of the imagination. If we confuse these two worlds of reality and imagination, then we breed not only national pride and religious fanaticism, but equally false philosophies and the dead art of the academies. We must surrender our minds to universal truth, but our imagination is free to dream; is as free as the dream; is the dream.[6]

In the dialectic between inner and outer reality, then, reason discovers truth and imagination creates beauty. We might diagram the process like this, where the direction of the arrows away from subjective reality indicates 'creation', and toward it 'discovery':

[5] *Ibid.*, pp. 124—125.
[6] *Ibid.*, p. 97.

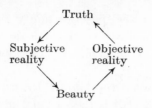

Seen in this way, there are two sides to the synthesis. The imaginative side, however, is prior to the rational. This priority stands out clearly if we oppose to the 'true' synthesis the 'false' one in which the rational and imaginative modes are directed wrongly. We can show this simply by reversing the direction of the arrows:

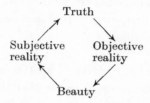

Here the rational side is prior. We create a logical, idealistic system which is not a discursive articulation of a 'direct communion' with the truth of reality, as it is in the 'true' synthesis. It is, rather, discursive and conceptual from the start, and so false. And the aesthetic side is equally false. First we construct conceptual systems, and then we find beauty in our conceptually articulated world and proceed to copy it. This is classical, or academic, art.

Read's poet-anarchist is both creator and discoverer; yet he avoids the mistake of attempting to create systems of thought or to discover beauty in that which already exists. Even so, however, his synthesis is always precarious. "I balance anarchism with surrealism, reason with romanticism, the understanding with the imagination, function with freedom", Read said. "The very delicacy and subtlety of the equilibrium is of its essence; for joy is only promised to those who strive to achieve it, and who, having achieved it, hold it lightly poised."[7] Thus the poet-anarchist remains, in the terminology of *Form in Modern Poetry*, a 'personality', attaining a balance that may from moment to moment be disrupted. He achieves what Read has called 'a certain order'; but how certain is forever uncertain. The 'false' synthesis, on the

---

[7] *Ibid.*, pp. 97—98.

other hand, provides the false certainty of ready-made order: the rigidity of "an arbitrary and idealistic system", the finality of "the dead art of the academies" – the kind of order which the 'character' needs.

The difference between the two syntheses, then, is a difference of priority. If we start with the rational mode, our philosophies have "no relation to reality", and our art is confined to "imitation'. But if we start with the imaginative mode, our art is freely created, in the sense of being the product of an aesthetic or intuitive insight into the nature of things, and our philosophies are grounded on the reality of this insight. The image has priority over the idea. Supporting the 'rational superstructure' of the mind is a more primitive structure where images hold mysterious sway. Discursive thought, which distinguishes subject and object, rests upon an aesthetic cognition which binds subject to object in a nondiscursive complex. Here, in this subjective-objective realm of 'superreality' is ultimate unity: the primordial images, the archetypes of the collective unconscious, merge into cosmic 'rhythm' and 'pattern' in a universal 'relatedness'. Accordingly, the ideas of the scientist and philosopher seem thin and derivative beside the profoundly significant images of the artist. Read concluded his essay, "Myth, Dream, and Poem", for example, by saying:

As a result of these experiments [his own dream-poems] poetry is seen more clearly than ever as the mediator between dream and reality. For centuries philosophy has been disintegrating this concept of reality, showing what a miserable compromise of averages and probabilities it represents. Philosophy falls back upon some form of idealism – some system of intellectual absolutes which gives coherence and continuity to existence; or it puts up with a provisional attitude like logical positivism, which is the contemporary form of agnosticism. But art is neither philosophy nor science, neither idealism nor agnosticism. It is an attempt to solve these existential problems by means of a living synthesis. Like the philosopher and the scientist, the poet experiences the contradictions of life, but instead of trying to solve them on the plane of inductive or deductive reasoning, solves them in the imagination. The imagination is the faculty by means of which we can encompass the antithetical terms of our experience, thus bringing the widest oppositions within a single focus, under a light which fuses them into a wholeness, a coherence, a plastic and sensuous integrity which is the work of art, that miracle which is the only objective evidence we possess of whatever superreality is cosmic and eternal.[8]

[8] Collected Essays, pp. 115–116.

The function of this 'miracle', this 'living synthesis', then, is to mediate between the finite and the infinite, the temporal and the eternal. The images of art – our 'only objective evidence' of the most ultimate of all knowledge – must therefore be sacred: they emerge from the profoundest depths of the self, and they relate us to the eternity of the cosmos.[9]

2

Involved in Read's neo-romanticism is a transformation of nineteenth-century romantic idealist aesthetics. The notion of the art work as a concrete embodiment of the Absolute had given to art a metaphysical sanction. But for Read, the twentieth-century romanticist, this sanction had been shorn away with the negation of idealism, and under the onslaught of empirical science art is subject to a progressive reduction. To prevent such an outcome, Read replaced the Idea, or Spirit, of idealist philosophy with a new absolute, the Superreal, which he believed is not a contradiction to empirical science but fully compatible with it. It was this transformation of idealism into superrealism that enabled him to balance a superreal realm against a real one. He could thus seem to be, in a sense, both idealist and realist. He could have a foot in each stream of thought and could appear now as the heir of Kant and Schelling, now of Aristotle and Aquinas. One could never be sure where he would turn up. Having transformed the Idea into the Image, he found it possible to claim the nineteenth-century idealist tradition while at the same time repudiating contemporary idealism. Croce's aesthetic, for example, which his own often resembles, he rejected as "the last flicker of a defunct

---

[9] Read's only work of prose fiction, *The Green Child* (London, 1935), is a complex, profound, and beautiful fantasy; a dialectical search for the meaning of life, in which inner and outer reality are held symbolically poised against each other. The story of Olivero's life in the world of action and event is folded within the story of his journey into the psyche, his search for his true self in the nontemporal realm of the green people, where he ultimately crystallizes in death into the structure of the universe. Read's allegory is rendered in images of such strange lustre, and with such perfection of prose, that the book is unforgettable.

idealism".[10] Read's whole attempt was to construct a post-idealist romanticism which could 'sanction' art and thus save it from scientific reductionism.

But if he can be said to have succeeded, it is only by means of an aesthetic reductionism that seems almost as bad as the scientific one. For where the work of art had been sanctioned in idealist romanticism as a manifestation of Spirit, an embodiment of the Ideal, all this is now turned around: it is the ideal and the spiritual that receive a sanction from the Image. After the 1930's Read's aesthetic reductionism became more evident with every book he published. In 1940 in *Annals of Innocence and Experience*, he confessed: "I have come to believe that the highest manifestation of the immanent will of the universe is the work of art."[11] In 1943 in *Education Through Art*, he referred to "the total nature of my claim", describing it this way: "I maintain that life itself, in its most secret and essential sources, is aesthetic – that it only *is* in virtue of the embodiment of energy in a form which is not merely material, but aesthetic."[12] And in subsequent writings, especially *Art and the Evolution of Man* (1951), *Icon and Idea* (1955), *The Forms of Things Unknown* (1960), and *The Origins of Form in Art* (1965), he attempted to demonstrate the priority of aesthetic over rational cognition, of the image over the idea. It is, Read believed, the image – in the sense of an approach to social organization, ethics, and education based on aesthetics – which can save us; and the idea – in the sense of a continued dominance of the rational, theoretical approach to these matters – which will destroy us. Only by a return to the secret, aesthetic sources of life can our technological revolution be brought under control, he argued, since the scientific philosophy which accompanied its rise has

[10] *Art Now* (New York, 1933), p. 53. Read of course owed something to Croce, as he admitted in *Annals of Innocence and Experience*, p. 214: "Croce's book *[Aesthetic]* was an essential stage in my development, but I never became a Crocean – some innate empiricism left me indifferent or uncomprehending before his idealism. The more I tended to accept his intuitional theory of art, the more baffled I became by his critical judgements, which seemed to proceed from a narrow classicism and even from a moral priggishness; until I concluded that he had always been a victim of his own environment."

[11] *Annals*, p. 10.

[12] *Education Through Art* (London, 1943), p. 35.

proved unable to cope with it. In his last thirty years Read became
an eloquent spokesman for an aesthetic philosophy of life, for
"art as a way of life".[13] But while we may agree with the justice of
many of his observations, we may also feel a legitimate disturbance
at his profound distrust for conceptual knowledge. He appeared
always preoccupied with finding ways to account for, and to
justify, the concept in terms of its aesthetic basis; there seemed on
his part almost an eagerness to lose the subject-object distinction,
to merge it back into a primal state of subjective-objective identity.
Similarly, the work of art in his theory tends to disappear in the
aesthetic cognition from which it emanates. Read's real concern
was not the work but the aesthetic principles which underlie it
and the universe, binding subject and object, microcosm and
macrocosm; principles of which the work is a miraculous proof
and exhibition.

The effect of his 'rehabilitation' of romanticism, then, seems far
from guaranteeing the poet's freedom, as he claimed. It is hard
to see how the subjective realm of art – "as free as the dream" –
is any more free than the objective realm of natural law it is meant
to balance against. If the artist's freedom lies in his daring to trans-
gress in his forms the mathematical patterns 'inherent in the universe', the truly creative part of this transgression, the 'miracle',
seems always to have occurred before the artist is given any actual
freedom at all. In his later work Read brought together ideas
drawn from a variety of sources – anthropology, Jungian psychoanalysis, Gestalt theory, Cassirer's philosophy of symbolic form,
Heidegger's metaphysics, Anton Ehrenzweig's theory of unconscious depth perception, and others – to establish a will-to-form
as a teleological principle, an impulse toward clarity and order
which urges man onward in his conquest of reality.

We cannot reconstruct or even imagine that "moment" in prehistory
when form first disclosed being, when man for the first time stabilized
being into the concreteness of a work of art . . . the origins of form in
art are also the origins of logos, of knowledge of being, of reality. Art,

[13] See especially Parts I and IV of The Forms of Things Unknown (London, 1960). Education Through Art remains an excellent source for Read's
general philosophy, especially the three chapters, "Unconscious Modes of
Integration", "The Natural Form of Education", and "The Aesthetic
Basis of Discipline and Morality" (Chapters VI, VII, VIII).

in so far as it has retained its primary function ... has throughout history always been such a mode of revelation.[14]

This primal ordering impulse is, indeed, the life force itself.

We are always threatened by spiritual and mental disintegration, the prelude to physical disintegration and death, and art is the effort to resist disintegration ... We cannot do this by thought, by intellection of any kind. Being can be disclosed only in an object, and the moment of disclosure is our awareness of the *logos* incorporated in the work of art.[15]

But the will to form seems to work blindly through a creative process over which the artist has no real control. The artist's conscious contributions to the process are never for Read a part of the primary process of formation. Read could not give the artist genuine freedom because he could not assign a creative role to the conscious intellect without contaminating the aesthetic mode of cognition with the rational. Thus in his theory the poem is always disappearing in the dream, criticism dissolving into sympathy, and the artist's freedom vanishing in the necessity of serving as a channel for the superreal Image.

The logic of Read's position is undeniable if we can accept his transformation of idealism into superrealism. Once a superrealist romanticism is established, with the Image functioning as an Absolute, we must expect the poet to offer us not an art of poetry but a knowledge of superreality. The spontaneity and irrationality of his images become the measure of their authenticity. Whatever we think of Read's position, we cannot call it inconsistent. But the consequence, as we have already observed, is that he must founder on the enormously difficult problem of poetic form. For the central terms of romantic theory, 'imagination' and 'organic form', have been shifted from an idealist to a superrealist basis. It may be, of course, that he was only pursuing these notions to their logical conclusion, and that romantic theory finds in the superreal Image its apotheosis. At any rate, he had to account for form within the limits of a radically altered conception of the poetic process. Let us look once more at his attempt to solve this problem.

[14] "The Origins of Form in the Plastic Arts", *The Origins of Form in Art* (London, 1965), p. 88.

[15] "The Disintegration of Form in Modern Art", *The Origins of Form in Art*, p. 187.

Like Coleridge, Read defined poetry in terms of imagination. But where for Coleridge the imaginative process was broadly creative, for Read it was narrowly aesthetic, and might more accurately be called 'imaging'. Coleridge described imagination as a 'synthetic' power which operated through the reconciliation of opposites: "the general with the concrete", "the idea with the image", "the individual with the representative", etc. It is thus a process in which the whole mind is engaged, and although mainly identified with poetry, it does not seem to exclude the processes of philosophy and science, insofar as these, too, are creative. But Read, having transformed idealism into superrealism, regarded the rational process as only a way of articulating or conceptualizing an intuitive, aesthetic knowledge that is already there. Its role, consequently, cannot be creative. The creative process is limited to a more primitive bodying forth of images – a moment of origination in which an equivalence is reached between what he called 'thought' and 'word'. In *English Prose Style* Read noted that Coleridge's definition of imagination is "couched in the terms of a transcendentalism which, to say the least of it (and the best), is no longer in fashion"; and he attempted to disengage the definition from its idealist assumptions and adapt it to his own purposes. This he did by rearranging Coleridge's distinction between the primary and secondary imagination to make the latter secondary in HIS sense:

The [Coleridge's] primary imagination is apparently identified with the general principle of creative thought, and the secondary imagination is that same creative principle in the degree that it becomes conscious activity. Later on in the *Biographia Literaria* it appears that imagination as defined here is largely identified with the poetic principle. With this identification I should agree in so far as imagination is a "creative" activity. In the moment of its origination the word is poetry. Let this be the primary sense of imagination. But then I think that in its secondary sense the word must be held to cover more factors than are implied in Coleridge's definition. Or rather, I think that some of the factors which Coleridge would describe as secondary are really primary, in that they are moments of origination or creativity; the secondary process is really the conscious arrangement of these moments into an expressive pattern.[16]

In this way Read made the primary and secondary imaginations differ in kind, in line with his distinction between creation and

[16] *English Prose Style* (London, 1928), p. 155.

construction. For Coleridge, however, the difference had been one of degree, as he had explicitly stated (in a passage which Read quoted): "The secondary Imagination I consider as an echo of the former [the primary], co-existing with the conscious will, yet still as identical with the primary in the *kind* of its agency, and differing in *degree*, and in the *mode* of its operation."[17] Read had radically transformed Coleridge. He had made it impossible for the 'conscious will' to be included in the poetic process, and so had closed the way from 'poetry' to 'poems' which Coleridge had attempted to keep open.

Consequently the notion of organic form becomes, as I pointed out earlier, quite a different thing in Read's hands from what it had been in Coleridge's, for deliberate art must now be excluded from any essential part in the forming process. Read never finally accounted for this process, I think, at least as it relates to the poetic medium. In the plastic arts perhaps he was more successful. His approach to the problem there was by way of that distinction between unconscious spontaneity and conscious deliberation we have noted so many times. It is a distinction between what might be called a primary 'forming' and a secondary 'making'. The moment of aesthetic cognition, if I understand Read rightly, is itself a moment of formation. He held that form is objective, in the sense that the principles of form are found throughout nature (although 'nature' includes also the human psyche); whereas content, by which he meant emotion, feeling, impulse, fantasy, and dream, is wholly subjective. In the creative moment, the subjective content 'finds' its inevitable form, thus binding inner and outer reality in a complex on a level below conscious deliberation.[18]

How this takes place remained in Read's theory of the plastic arts always mysterious. He said in one essay, " . . . we find ourselves manipulating a few simple forms, which are the predetermined forms of visual significance. The psychic content of art has to fit into these predetermined forms, like jelly into a mould."[19] But this seems an unfortunate metaphor for the process (more than

---

[17] *Ibid.*, p. 154.

[18] See *Education Through Art*, Chapter II, "The Definition of Art", and Chapter VI, "Unconscious Modes of Integration".

[19] "The Creative Process", *The Forms of Things Unknown*, p. 61. Originally published as "The Dynamics of Art", *Eranos Jahrbuch 1952* (Zurich, 1953).

a little reminiscent of Coleridge's 'mechanic' form), and later in the same essay Read searched for another: "In comparing form to a mould into which the artist pours a certain content I have ignored the important fact that it is the artist who discovers the form . . . The form is found by instinct, ready at hand like a glove already shaped by personal use . . ."[20] This metaphor is better, if only because it reveals the forming process as finally inexplicable. In the plastic arts there was for Read no objective content to be shaped and fitted. Thus the representation of objective reality, and the skills requisite to this undertaking, are quite beside the point. The form-content problem is really abolished: content is from its inception already 'formed'; it emerges as form. If the artist then deliberately uses his skills to elaborate his images, the result is that inversion of the classical form-content view we have noted before. In a plastic medium this theory is at least comprehensible, although to make it work Read had, in effect, to rule out must of the classical and renaissance tradition in western art.[21] In the verbal medium of poetry, however, the difficulties seem insuperable. To banish an objective content from poetry it is necessary to rid the poem of discourse, to render it nondiscursive by 'freeing' the poetic image. The subjective content can then find its 'equivalence' in the image, while the 'art' of poetry, which for Read was mostly a 'prose' art, is relegated to the academies. But the fact is that once the poetic image has been cut loose from discourse, there is, theoretically, no satisfactory POETIC form to be found for it because poetry is a temporal, not a spatial, art.

Read never solved the problem of the temporality of poetic form. He began by viewing rhythm as a 'decoration' for the image, but this was unsatisfactory because it had the effect of excluding rhythm from the forming process.[22] His next step, therefore, was

---

[20] *Ibid.*, p. 62.

[21] This tradition Read called 'humanistic', or 'academic', as well as 'classical'. It falls outside "art properly so-called" because it has an objective content. Humanistic art imitates the appearance of an objective world, or it illustrates an idea, and it performs these functions only at the cost of contamination by the discursive reason. True art remained for Read always as free as possible of such contamination, and it is, he believed, the great achievement of modern art to have exploited this freedom. See especially *Art Now* and *The Origins of Form in Art*.

[22] See above, pp. 24—25.

to try to separate the instinctual basis of rhythm from its conscious elaboration into metrical patterns.[23] Thus to the question of what poetic form the 'freed' image takes, his answer was 'free verse' – the rhythm of 'sincerity'. In *Form in Modern Poetry* he had relatively little to say about rhythm; it was the 'fusing' of 'structure' and 'content' he was concerned with, and it was to this that he attempted to apply Coleridge's notion of organic form. In 1953, however, in *The True Voice of Feeling*, he identified organic form in poetry specifically with rhythm. In this book Coleridge's notion of 'form as proceeding' versus 'shape as superinduced' means that poetic rhythm should arise directly from the emotional situation of the poet rather than from conformity to a pre-established metrical pattern. "The pulse of the thought", Read said (adapting a remark of Coleridge's), "is the beat in the rhythm."[24] Consequently the test of the poet's 'sincerity', and thus of the genuiness of his poetry, is his rhythm. Read set out in *The True Voice of Feeling* to trace Coleridge's organic principle in the rhythm of poets from Wordsworth to T. S. Eliot. In his argument he encompassed Coleridge, Wordsworth, Keats, Hopkins, Whitman and Lawrence; and he had of course no trouble in showing a progression away from metrical regularity and toward a closer relationship with colloquial speech. But when he arrived at T. E. Hulme, the theoretician of the Imagist school who attempted to 'free' the poetic image from discourse, he reached a crux. For it turns out that 'free verse' was for Read the fulfillment of Coleridge's organic principle, and furthermore that it is wholly bound up with the 'isolation' of the poetic image which he saw as the distinguishing mark of modern poetry. (He rejected Whitman's and Lawrence's free verse as mostly a false kind.) Read admitted there was a crux for his argument here. For where Coleridge had been suspicious of the image as a cognitive instrument, being convinced that the 'best parts' of language were the more abstract and general, Hulme saw those same parts as 'worn counters' and the poet's task as the renewal of language through the creation of images. Thus, if there is a continuity of development from Coleridge to Hulme, it is a continuity that involves a radical transformation by means of which the image takes precedence over the idea. As Read said,

[23] See above, pp. 62–63.
[24] *The True Voice of Feeling* (London, 1953), pp. 23–25.

Hulme was the first to realize that the coherence of the poem, its scape and inscape, was not necessarily a logical coherence. The poem had been released, by that development we have traced from Coleridge to Hopkins to become a "universe" of its own. Hulme made it clear that such universes are made, not of empty booming words, but of plastic images, words impressed like clay with the poet's invention. It is not merely a question of importing images into the stream of discourse, to make it more vivid. Poetry is rather a crystallization of the discourse into symbolic images. But even this statement might be held to imply that discourse, grammatical language, in some sense is there first, and that the poet is merely the agent of a transformation. What is there first, said Hulme, is the world in its concreteness, evident to the senses: the physical phenomena. The poet seizes these, finds their verbal equivalence, and the rest – beauty, significance, metaphysical reverberations– is there as an intrinsic grace. Thought begins with the simultaneous presentation to the mind of two distinct but related images. Poetry is what then *happens*. Prose is a post-mortem on the event.[25]

Poetry, then, is something which 'happens' through the juxtaposition of images; and prose, or discursive thought, is confined to the investigation of this 'event'. Thus the universe of the poem is altogether different from the universe of prose, and it need not rely for its principle of coherence on the 'stream of discourse'. But if this is the case, in what sense can we say, in Read's (and Coleridge's) phrase, that "the pulse of the thought is the beat in the rhythm"? It seems evident that for Coleridge this 'pulse' and this 'beat' were linked to the 'stream of discourse'. And indeed it is hard to conceive of them in any other way. Read spoke of imagist 'thought' in terms of a non-temporal 'crystallization', rather than a temporal 'stream'; but how such 'thought' can have a 'pulse', and such 'crystallization' a 'beat', is never explained. All we are given is 'free verse', the culmination of a historical development away from metrical regularity. Yet it would appear that rhythm, no matter how organic and 'sincere', could never be Read's final test for poetry; for in the isolated image – visual, static, plastic – he had a spatial principle of form that supersedes the temporal principle. When his absolute distinction between poetry and prose is pressed, it seems the decision must finally be, as it was in *English Prose Style*, that poetry may be 'without rhythm'; that it can 'inhere' in a single word, "even a single syllable", while prose "always has rhythm of some kind". In the last analysis, Read retained

[25] *Ibid.*, pp. 114—115.

from the 'art' of poetry only diction – not a conventional poetic
diction, of course, but the direct, immediate diction of 'sincerity',
the verbal equivalence of vision. It is to the mysterious moment
when feeling equates with image that Coleridge's organic principle
was narrowed by. Read, and how that moment becomes a poem
he was never able to show. For him to have invoked Coleridge
here means to pass over Coleridge's considered views of the poetic
process in favor of his description of the production of *Kubla Khan*,
disregarding the fact that he offered that poem as a 'literary
curiosity' and "not for any supposed *poetic* merit".[26]

3

What we are dealing with here, as we observed earlier, is the
'form' of a cognitive process, not the form of a poem, and this
determined Read's entire critical attitude, which was always
oriented toward the process rather than the poem. In his last
years he elaborated his account of the poetic process in essays of
a depth and power that can scarcely be suggested by a synopsis,
enriched as these writings are with the learning and experience
of a lifetime. But I can see no change in his view of the process.
To account for poetry is to account for the 'shaping power' that
forms images.

> ... we must ask what trigger mechanism releases any particular
> image from the brain and sends it into the stream of consciousness ...
> it must be an intensification of feeling, which results in an apperception
> of value: a vague feeling-tone becomes concrete, acquires direction and
> is precipitated into consciousness as an image. But the odd thing is that
> the image ... enters consciousness fully formed, effective by reason
> of its form. What agency, behind consciousness, has had this formative
> function? ... We assume that the brain is a system of physical molecules,
> but I think we must suppose that it is also a system of mental facts or
> monads – that the infinite store of impressions fed into the brain by
> sensations is automatically sorted into *Gestalten*, metaphysical config-
> urations of infinite significance and vitality.
>   ... between the feeling and work of art there is a force *(mana:* the
> "energy proper to the poet") which fuses the impressions of sense into

---

[26] I do not suggest that Read was unaware of this difficulty. See *The
True Voice of Feeling*, p. 23.

formal and significant images . . . Such images, in their purity, are the primary elements in poetry and all the arts.

. . . it is the *mana* we identify with the source of life itself, which is formative in its deepest recesses. To the extent that we allow our sensibility to be guided by this shaping power . . . and exclude all judgements and prejudices proceeding from the ego . . .to that extent we are true poets and worthy to receive the truth revealed by the Muse.[27]

This may account for poetry as 'sensuous thought',[28] but it is just as difficult as ever to see how it accounts for a poem. Read appeared still to assume that the problem could be surmounted by emphasizing the concreteness of the process, the objectivity of this exploration of subjectivity. The poetic process, he said, is "not a stream of feeling carrying words in a predetermined direction" but an "autonomous verbal activity trying to establish a concrete form . . . which may afterwards be identified . . . with a feeling or state of mind".[29] We may even agree that the poetic process presents "to the mind a self which the poet afterwards gratefully accepts as his own",[30] while we still wonder how it presents him with a poem.

And in these later writings Read came no closer to an accommodation with the contextualist approach of the new criticism than he had before. His credo still seemed to be as he had stated it in 1950 in "The Critic as Man of Feeling": the basis of criticism is sympathy, and analysis is always a secondary activity. Thus the critic can do little more than "announce the presence" of the highest qualities in a work:

It is doubtful if the qualities that give Homer, Dante and Shakespeare their supremacy can be analyzed by lesser minds. The *accent* of high seriousness, said Arnold (and he was wise to call it an accent) comes from absolute sincerity. That is true, but how do we define sincerity? We should not make the attempt. We recognize, we *feel*, such a quality, and if such an action seems like an abdication of the critical intelligence, I can only suggest that there are in the House of Art certain tabernacles which the critic should enter with lowered eyelids, so dazzling is their glory.[31]

[27] "The Poet and his Muse", *The Origins of Form in Art*, pp. 142—145.

[28] "See The Creative Experience in Poetry", *The Forms of Things Unknown*, p. 134. See also "Poetic Consciousness" in the same book.

[29] "The Poet and his Muse", *loc. cit.*, p. 132.

[30] *Ibid.*

[31] I quote from the reprint of this essay, "The Faith of a Critic", in *The Tenth Muse*, pp. 327—328.

From the contextualist standpoint this is indeed an "abdication of the critical intelligence". For Read, however, it was a necessary consequence. Since poetry is a cognitive process in which the discursive intelligence is denied any essential role, criticism must first of all involve an instinctive judgment on the genuineness or falsity of this process. Whatever else it may involve is subsidiary. For contextualism, on the other hand, the poetic act is supremely conscious, technique is fully creative, and analysis is therefore the primary critical activity. The poem is a centripetal structure whose elements cohere through tensions, particularly of irony and paradox; the critical intelligence, with great subtlety, probes and reveals the complexity of the structure, which is finally the measure of its value. But different as this approach is from Read's it nonetheless assumes a view of the cognitive character of poetry much like his. For with contextualism there is the same insistence that the poet offer a knowledge closed to 'prose', or scientific, discourse; the difference is that the poet must create or discover this knowledge through the complexity of his linguistic means. We may object, however, that the extreme complication of the poet's statement is not sufficient to give it the status of a unique knowledge. If, in other words, the cognitive process of poetry differs only in DEGREE of complexity from the process of prose, how can it yield a different KIND of knowledge? Whatever our doubts about Read may be, we are at least in no doubt on this point. He insisted that if the poet offers us another kind of knowledge, it must be by virtue of another kind of cognitive process. And it follows that we will recognize him not by probing the complexity of his linguistic means – they may indeed be very simple – but by a more passive, receptive activity: listening for an accent of absolute sincerity.[32]

[32] The best critical study of Read written from the contextualist standpoint is Solomon Fishman's "Sir Herbert Read: Poetics vs. Criticism", loc. cit. Fishman agrees generally with Read's view of the cognitive character of poetry, but argues that Read's insistence on sympathy, rather than analysis, as the basis of criticism resulted in his poetics "overcoming" his criticism: he dissolved criticism by merging it with the poem. Fishman's argument revolves around the issue of whether technique is creative. He claims that technique, "in the significant sense, is itself a mode of knowledge" (p. 162). He appears, finally, to be baffled by Read. What he fails to perceive, I think, is that for Read technique is the WRONG mode of knowledge: it is not POETIC knowledge. In a graceful rejoinder to Fishman, Journal of Aesthetics and Art Criticism, XIII (3, 1955), p. 408, Read discussed

4

Read's final concern was always with a theoretical superreal poetry against which actual poems must fall short, and he could seldom look at the contemporary poetic scene without becoming painfully aware of the discrepancy. The years just before and after the First World War became for him almost a poetic golden age, the moment of an historic attempt to purify English poetry, to rid it of contamination with discursive, analytical modes of thought. The effort made then to free the image from discourse made it seem as significant a moment in the history of English poetry as the appearance of Wordsworth's and Coleridge's *Lyrical Ballads* in 1798. He saw little but a slow falling-off after the early 1920's, a falling-off that became catastrophic during the 1930's when poets were seduced into political allegiances. In 1939 he discussed the younger British poets, especially Auden, Day Lewis, MacNeice, and Spender, from the standpoint of "one whose practice in the art was formed a quarter century ago". He deplored these poets' habit of (in Mathew Arnold's phrase) "thinking aloud" in verse. "Thinking aloud", he said, was "merely a continuous flow of associated ideas, and for that reason it may well be rich in similes and metaphors; and for such a process rhyming is an obvious aid." To this he contrasted the poetic ideal of his own generation:

The new ideal, which we called Imagism, was what we can now recognize as the eternal aesthetic ideal – an ideal of form, indifferent to the nature of the subject-matter . . . What was aimed at, by means of precision of expression and vitality of image, was above all an aesthetic entity – a poem, that is to say, which had a clear crystalline objectivity, due to sincerity of feeling, exactness of expression, and the consequent virtues of precision, economy and vividness. Pound and a little later Eliot accepted and furthered these ideals; D. H. Lawrence was well within their range; and I do not think that as ideals they have ever

---

the genesis of forms from the standpoint of psychoanalysis and Gestalt psychology, and remarked: "I must protest that I do not dismiss technique; but technique must not be conceived as a surface treatment of inspiration: it is the process of formation itself." What this means is that technique, to be valid for Read, must be merged with inspiration as a 'process of formation', *i.e.*, be something which can go on below the level of conscious control. It cannot be a MEANS without being a "surface treatment of inspiration".

been renounced by the poets of my generation. In due course they were reintegrated in the ideals of surrealist poetry . . .[33]

It is in the light of this contrast between image and discourse, or vision and rhetoric, that Read continued to see his younger contemporaries. He found it hard to understand why, with a few exceptions (particularly Dylan Thomas), they had not followed their elders. In the preface to a new edition of *Form in Modern Poetry* in 1948, he said: "Why a later generation should have refused to follow where we led is no doubt a phase of history which some devotee of the dialectical method will one day explain . . . One can only conclude that these poets have never stood where we stand, nor seen what we see, nor felt as we feel."[34]

Yet even in 1918 Read was complaining about his contemporaries – even about the Imagists themselves. The Imagists, he said then, "betray a pitiful lack of that aesthetic selection which is the artist's most peculiar duty".[35] And his satisfaction with Pound and Eliot was mixed with so many qualifications and regrets that one wonders if these poets indeed ever stood, or saw, or felt as he did. (Certainly it is hard to imagine either of them proposing the ideals of surrealist poetry as a 'reintegration' of his own poetic ideals.) In *The True Voice of Feeling* Read credited Pound with having formulated 'the basic principles of modern poetry' in 1915, when he was associated with the Imagists.[36] His work thereafter Read saw as being increasingly filled with 'defections' and 'corruptions'. The *Cantos*, he decided finally, are 'incoherent'[37] (although what kind of coherence for the long poem Read's own theory provides has never been clear). Read's criticism of Eliot in *The True Voice of Feeling* centered on Eliot's conception of 'verse' as a medium existing somewhere between poetry and prose. What this means is that Eliot still refused to make an absolute distinction between poetry and prose; he saw them, rather, as grading into each other through a third medium, verse, which is neither the one nor the other. Poetry he called a 'point of inten-

---

[33] "The Present State of Poetry in England", *Kenyon Review*, I. 4 (1939), 360.

[34] *Form in Modern Poetry* (London, 1948), p. iv.

[35] See above, p. 26.

[36] *The True Voice of Feeling*, pp. 126—127.

[37] *Ibid.*, p. 135.

sity'; verse he found a useful medium for the playwright. For Read, however, poetry was not something the poet can slip into and out of: as a mental state, a certain tension of the mind, it either exists or it does not. He would settle for nothing less than a poetry consisting WHOLLY of that "point of intensity at which the force of the emotions fuses the utterance to a glowing heat". With poetry, Read said in this book, we cross a line which divides the discursive from the nondiscursive, and our apprehension must be through a kind of intelligence different from the rational: "Poetry is non-discursive: which does not mean that it cannot be apprehended by the intelligence. Intelligence, in the sense in which the word has been used by philosophers like Plato, Spinoza and Bergson, includes as an active component the liveliness of the sensibility, a feeling for the heights and depths, the contours, the *Gestalt* of communication."[38] Consequently, Read doubted Eliot's entire project of writing for the theatre, with the "surrender to the public demand for discursive means of communication" which it entails. He questioned whether it is possible for poetry and drama to be united, since "drama has always been indissolubly attached to action". He questioned their union even in Shakespeare:

> Poetry is essentially a quality, an abstract quality evoked by concrete images, and Shakespeare is an imperfect dramatist precisely because the poetry keeps breaking in, suspending the action for its moment of existence. There are some areas of consciousness which the poet can only enter if he renounces action, and it is difficult to see how the notion of a perfect union of drama and poetry can remain other than the mirage which Mr. Eliot has until now had before his eyes.[39]

But Eliot's persistence in writing for the theatre was, as we saw before, part of his refusal to theorize himself away from the poetic medium and the poetic audience. Because he refused to make the kind of absolute distinctions Read insisted upon, he could retain the conception of a poetic art flexible enough to have a number of uses. Once we make those distinctions, however, we are at Read's cross-roads and must choose either/or. And if we choose 'poetry' we find we have chosen an essence, an 'abstract quality', rather than an art. It is no wonder Read found a falling-off everywhere he looked. In *The True Voice of Feeling*, his satisfaction seemed

[38] *Ibid.*, pp. 148—149.
[39] *Ibid.*, p. 149.

greatest in the chapter on Hulme. Yet Hulme was a theoretician first and a poet second. It was not Hulme's ingenious little poems which delighted Read; it was his theoretical 'isolation' of the image. Read measured practicing poets against the notion of a superreal modern poetry absolutely uncontaminated with discourse, and a lost golden age in which it was created. Such a notion, I believe, is a myth – evidently a sustaining and nourishing myth for Read, but a myth all the same. And the consequence was that actual poetry seemed more or less corrupt to him. He once remarked that he was aided in experiencing the poetic 'shock' by the 'extra veil' of a foreign language.

> Rilke in one of his poems cries:
>> Singe die Gärten, mein Herz, die du nicht kennst;
>> wie in Glas eingegossene Gärten, klar, unerreichbar.
>
> And that is the perfect analysis of the sensation: the vision of an unknown garden, embedded in glass, clear but unattainable. Vision without meaning, concrete, synthetic, but held in suspense, contemplated without question.[40]

This was exactly Read's poetic ideal – 'vision without meaning' – and it is of course more easily realized when the foreignness of a language throws a certain opacity over 'meaning'. In one's own language, 'meaning' gets in the way and the vision becomes corrupt. In 1955 as he summed up an account of English poetry since the First World War, Read appeared almost to have lost hope:

> I have been sparing of names in this survey of the drift of twentieth-century poetry, but let us look back across the chart for a moment. There was one clear line of progress – the isolation and clarification of the image, and the perfection of a diction that would leave the image unclouded by rhetoric or sentiment. To that task our greatest poets – Yeats, Pound, Eliot and Thomas – devoted their best energies. But now there is a failure of nerve: eyes are dazzled, diffidence falters, and once again a veil of rhetoric is drawn over the vision of the poet. Sentiment supersedes sensation, the poetic consciousness is corrupted. Many individual voices rise again in the dusk. Yeats dead, Pound silenced, Eliot lost to the theatre, Thomas gone before his time – it is the hour of the twittering machines. We listen to them as we drink our martinis or smoke a cigarette, and for an hour or two we feel content. Then the night comes and there is no voice to fill the silence.[41]

---

[40] "Obscurity in Poetry", *Collected Essays in Literary Criticism*, p. 91.
[41] "The Drift of Modern Poetry", *Encounter*, IV (1, 1955), 10. Reprinted as "The Image in Modern English Poetry", in *The Tenth Muse*, pp. 117–138.

Here, then, everyone has fallen away, and it seems almost as if Read, left alone, was himself the last uncorrupted poetic consciousness.

5

Again one cannot avoid reflecting that a formalist aesthetic works better with the plastic arts, where form can exist in some degree of purity, where the image can truly be SEEN. And it may be that Read's critical, historical, and philosophical work in the field of these arts will be viewed eventually as his major accomplishment. The list of his books devoted wholly or largely to the plastic arts and published since 1950 is impressively long,[42] and common to them all is the theme he announced in 1918 in his first statement of poetic theory; the significance of form. This theme he explored in these books with great virtuosity, deepening and widening his argument for the biological and teleological function of art. But it is evident, I think, that he did not have an equivalent success in applying a formalist aesthetic to poetry. He acknowledged the difficulties involved:

The very fact that poetry makes use of words, the material also of rational discourse, complicates any discussion of its non-rational uses; though I believe that the kind of illumination that comes to the consciousness of the poet, and is expressed in words, is not essentially different from the kind of illumination that comes to the painter or sculptor and is expressed in visual images . . .[43]

And again: "It is possible that the function of form is not so evident in the art of literature as in the visual arts, but that is an illusion arising from the more acute 'semblance' . . . of the visual

---

[42] *Art and the Evolution of Man* (London, 1951); *Contemporary British Art* (London, 1951); *The Philosophy of Modern Art* (London, 1953); *Icon and Idea* (Cambridge, Mass., 1955); *The Art of Sculpture* (New York, 1956); *The Tenth Muse* (London, 1958); *A Concise History of Modern Painting* (London, 1959); *The Forms of Things Unknown* (London, 1960); *A Letter to a Young Painter* (London, 1962); *A Concise History of Modern Sculpture* (London, 1964); *The Origins of Form in Art* (London, 1965); *Art and Alienation* (London, 1967).

[43] "Art as a Symbolic Language", *The Forms of Things Unknown*, p. 38.

arts.''[44] Yet perhaps the difference is not an 'illusion'. The recalcitrance of the poetic medium in accommodating to a formalist aesthetic may be due to its impurity, its stubborn connection to a realm of discourse where words and sentences 'mean', to a world of flesh and blood, to what Donald Davie has called ''the reek of the human''.[45] The 'divine indifference'[46] Read sought in the image may not finally be obtainable from a linguistic medium.

And perhaps even in the plastic arts formalist developments have nearly run their course, and the great line of achievement Read traced in his books on modern art is coming to an end. It may be significant, at any rate, that he (always previously the apostle of the new) repudiated the newest art as a 'disintegration of form' and a betrayal of the movement that began with Cézanne. ''This art without concentration, without relationship, this art which boasts of its inconsequence and incoherence, is not art at all . . .''.[47] The note of despair one hears in Read's last books was, I think, not caused solely by the precarious state of civilization – ''I see everywhere the threatening shadow of catastrophe that overtakes a people without vision''[48] – and the apparent hopelessness of his aim to bring a renewal through aesthetics; it was connected also with his disturbance over the direction the plastic arts were taking. He was unable to see the will to form, the teleological urge toward formal clarity, order and integrity in the latest developments in these arts. Their ''incoherence, insensitivity, brutality, and privacy'' he described as the betrayal of a sacred trust.

The whole purpose of art as a creative and cognitive activity is called in question. What we are witnessing is not merely the disintegration of form in art, but the disintegration of intelligence itself, a descent into the eternal ''fun fair'' which is neither funny nor fair, but an inferno into which the intellectually alienated and morally insensitive

---

[44] ''The Faith of a Critic'', *Poetry and Experience* (London, 1967), p. 16. This is a new essay under (confusingly enough) a title used before (in *The Tenth Muse*). Also in this volume are three essays from *Reason and Romanticism* previously unreprinted – ''The Definition of Comedy'', ''The Disciples of Diderot'', and '' The Dialogue'' – and a rewritten version of ''The Attributes of Criticism'' from the same book.

[45] *Articulate Energy*, p. 165.

[46] *Poetry and Experience*, p. 117.

[47] ''The Disintegration of Form in Modern Art'', *loc. cit.*, p. 187.

[48] *The Forms of Things Unknown*, p. 12.

vandals of an urban economy descend in their ruthless search for any object on which to expend their destructive energies.[49]

Particularly disturbing was the notion that he himself, who had played a not inconsiderable role in the establishment and promulgation of modern art, might bear some of the blame for its disintegration.

To what extent are we critics responsible for the present nihilistic phase of art? Is it a logical consequence of all we have striven for in the past fifty years? Does the movement that began with Cézanne and his resolve to wrest the secret of being from the visible universe lead logically and inevitably to the present disintegration of the visual image? I would wear sackcloth and ashes if I thought so.[50]

He did not seem to consider the possibility that the formalist movement, like any movement in the arts, contained from the beginning the seeds of its own demise. For Read, what began with Cézanne in the plastic arts, like what began with the Imagists in poetry, was not really a 'movement' at all; it was simply art itself.

Read will take his place finally as a great theorist of the formalist movement in the arts of the twentieth-century West. In English literary criticism he was the true heir of T. E. Hulme, whose combination of Bergson's and Worringer's ideas created a formalist poetic. Read's particular virtue lay in clarifying this poetic by pushing its implications to their furthest extreme. In the work of no other contemporary critic do we find the cognitive character of poetry established with such authority; yet it is done only by leading us away from poetic art to a superreal poetry which art would destroy. Our recognition of Read's sensitivity and perceptiveness, and our gratitude for the valuable insights he gave us over the years, do not make his conclusions any easier to accept. But we should bear in mind that those conclusions are not illogical if we can accept his starting point: poetry as a mode of cognition, a kind of knowledge. It is therefore the starting point itself that his work brings into question. We can say of his criticism, as he said of his poetry, that one need not approach it with "squared shoulders": one can accept or reject him "on the instant". The fact is, however, that he developed the logic of his position

---

[49] "The Disintegration of Form in Modern Art", loc. cit., p. 182.
[50] Ibid., p. 186.

in such a way as to make it very difficult to reject him without rejecting his starting point. And since it is from this point that a great deal of contemporary criticism begins, his presence on the critical scene was always somewhat disturbing. To study his development, to see how he reached his conclusions, serves, I think, to clear the air, to bring us up short against the real issues in the doctrine of poetry as knowledge.

SELECTED BIBLIOGRAPHY

Aquinas, St. Thomas, The "Summa Theologica" of St. Thomas Aquinas, Part I. Literally translated by Fathers of the English Dominican Province (London, Burns, Oates & Washbourne, Ltd., n.d.).

Bell, Clive, Art (New York, Capricorn Books, 1958).

Benda, Julien, The Betrayal of the Intellectuals, Introduction by Herbert Read (Boston, Beacon Press, 1955).

Berry, Francis, Herbert Read ("Writers and Their Work", No. 45) (London, Longmans, Green & Co., 1945).

Coffman, Stanley K., Jr. Imagism: A Chapter for the History of Modern Poetry (Norman, University of Oklahoma Press, 1951).

Coleridge, S. T., Biographia Literaria, Edited by J. Shawcross, 2 vols. (London, Oxford University Press, 1907).

—, Shakespearean Criticism, Edited by T. M. Raysor, 2 vols. (London, J. M. Dent & Sons, 1960).

D'Arcy, M. C., S. J., "The Thomistic Synthesis and Intelligence", Criterion, VI, 3 (September, 1927), 210—228.

Davie, Donald, Articulate Energy: An Inquiry into the Syntax of English Poetry (London, Routledge & Kegan Paul, 1955).

Eliot, T. S., "The Idea of a Literary Review", Criterion, IV, 1 (January, 1926), 1—6.

—, "Mr. Middleton Murry's Synthesis", Criterion, VI, 4 (October, 1927), 340—347.

—, Review of Reason and Romanticism by Herbert Read, Criterion, IV, 4 (October, 1926), 751—757.

—, Selected Essays: 1917—1932 (New York, Harcourt, Brace & Co., 1932).

—, The Use of Poetry and the Use of Criticism: Studies in the Relation of Criticism to Poetry in England (London, Faber & Faber, 1933).

Fernandez, Ramon, "A Note on Intelligence and Intuition", Criterion, VI, 4 (October, 1927), 332—339.

Fishman, Solomon, "Sir Herbert Read: Poetics vs. Criticism", Journal of Aesthetics and Art Criticism, XIII, 2 (December, 1954), 156—162.

Flint, F. S., Otherworld: Cadences (London, The Poetry Bookshop, 1920).

Frank, Joseph, "Spatial Form in Modern Literature", in Criticism: The Foundations of Modern Literary Judgement, Edited by Mark Schorer, Josephine Miles, and Gordon McKenzie (New York, Harcourt, Brace & Co., 1958).

Freud, Sigmund, *A General Introduction to Psychoanalysis* (Garden City, Doubleday & Co., 1953).

—, *New Introductory Lectures on Psycho-analysis*, Translated by W. J. Sprott (London, The Hogarth Press, 1949).

Häusermann, H. W., "The Development of Herbert Read", in *Herbert Read: an introduction to his work by various hands*, Edited by Henry Treece (London, Faber & Faber, 1944).

Hough, Graham, *Image and Experience: Studies in a Literary Revolution* (London, Gerald Duckworth & Co., Ltd., 1960).

Hulme, T. E., *Speculations: Essays on Humanism and the Philosophy of Art*, Edited by Herbert Read (London, Routledge & Kegan Paul, 1924).

Jung, C. G., *Psychological Types: The Psychology of Individuation*, Translated by H. C. Baynes (London, Routledge & Kegan Paul, 1924).

Kermode, Frank, *Romantic Image* (London, Routledge & Kegan Paul, 1957).

Maritain, Jacques, *Bergsonian Philosophy and Thomism* (New York, Philosophical Library, 1955).

Muller, Herbert J., *Science and Criticism: The Humanistic Tradition in Contemporary Thought* (New Haven, Yale University Press, 1943).

Murry, J. Middleton, "Concerning Intelligence", *Criterion*, VI, 6 (December, 1927), 524—533.

—, "Reason and Criticism", *Times Literary Supplement*, July 8, 1926, 453—454.

—, "Towards a Synthesis", *Criterion*, V, 3 (June, 1927), 294—313.

Pound, Ezra, *Literary Essays of Ezra Pound*, Edited with an Introduction by T. S. Eliot (London, Faber & Faber, 1954).

Read, Herbert, *Annals of Innocence and Experience* (London, Faber & Faber, 1940. Revised ed., 1946).

—, *Art and Alienation: The Role of the Artist in Society* (London, Thames and Hudson, 1967).

—, *Art and the Evolution of Man* (London, Freedom Press, 1951).

—, *Art and Industry: The Principles of Industrial Design* (London, Faber & Faber, 1934. Revised ed., 1953).

—, *Art and Society* (New York, MacMillan Co., 1937); (Revised ed. New York, Pantheon Books, 1945).

—, *Art Now: An Introduction to the Theory of Modern Painting and Sculpture* (London, Faber & Faber, 1933); (Revised ed. New York, Pitman Publishing Co., 1948).

—, *The Art of Sculpture* (New York, Pantheon Books, 1956).

—, *A Coat of Many Colours: Occasional Essays* (London, George Routledge & Sons, 1945).

—, *Collected Essays in Literary Criticism* (London, Faber & Faber, 1938. Revised ed., 1951).

—, *A Concise History of Modern Painting* (London, Thames and Hudson, 1959).

—, *A Concise History of Modern Sculpture* (London, Thames and Hudson, 1964).

—, "The Critic as Man of Feeling", *Kenyon Review*, XII, 4 (1950), 575—580.

—, *The Cult of Sincerity* (London, Faber & Faber, 1968).

—, "Definitions Towards a Modern Theory of Poetry", *Art and Letters*, I, 3 (January, 1918), 73—78.

—, "The Dethronement of Descartes", *Times Literary Supplement*, September 9, 1926, 585—586.

—, "The Drift of Modern Poetry", *Encounter*, IV. 1 (1955).

—, "The Dynamics of Art", in *Eranos Jahrbuch 1952*, Band XXI. Herausgegeben von Olga Fröbe-Kapteyn (Zurich, Rhein-Verlag, 1953).

—, *Education Through Art* (New York, Pantheon Books, 1943).

—, *English Prose Style* (London, G. Bell & Sons, 1928); (Revised ed. New York, Pantheon Books, 1952).

—, *English Stained Glass* (London and New York, G. P. Putnam's Sons, 1926).

—, *Form in Modern Poetry* (New York, Sheed & Ward, 1933); (Revised ed. London, Vision, 1948).

—, "The Form of Modern Poetry", *Symposium*, I, 3 (July, 1930), 293—309).

—, *The Forms of Things Unknown: Essays Towards an Aesthetic Philosophy* (London, Faber & Faber, 1960).

—, "The Future of Poetry", *Times Literary Supplement*, September 10, 1925, 573—574.

—, *The Green Child: A Romance* (London, William Heinemann, 1935).

—, "Humanism and the Absolute (The Texts of a Debate)", *Criterion*, VIII, 31 (December,1928), 270—276.

—, *Icon and Idea: The Function of Art in the Development of Human Consciousness* (Cambridge, Harvard University Press, 1955).

—, "The Implications of Behaviorism", *Criterion*, VII, 4 (June, 1928), 64—75.

—, *In Defence of Shelley & Other Essays* (London, William Heinemann, 1936).

—, *Julien Benda and the New Humanism* (Seattle, University of Washington Book Store, 1930).

—, *A Letter to a Young Painter* (London, Thames and Hudson, 1962).

—, *The Meaning of Art* (London, Faber & Faber, 1931); (Revised ed. New York, Pitman Publishing Co., 1951).

—, "Myth, Dream, and Poem", *transition*, no. 27 (1938).

—, "The Nature of Metaphysical Poetry", *Criterion*, I, 3 (April 1923), 246—266.

—, "A Neglected Aspect of Edgar Allan Poe", *Art and Letters*, II, 3 (Summer, 1919), 137—141.

—, *The Origins of Form in Art* (London, Thames and Hudson, 1965).

—, "Personality in Literature", *Symposium*, II. 3 (July, 1931).

—, *Phases of English Poetry* (London, Hogarth Press, 1928).

—, *The Philosophy of Modern Art* (New York, Horizon Press, 1953).

—, *Poetry and Anarchism* (London, Faber & Faber, 1938).

—, *Poetry and Experience* (London, Vision Press, 1967).

—, "The Present State of Poetry in England", *Kenyon Review*, I. 4 (1939), 359—369.

—, "Psycho-analysis and the Critic", *Criterion*, III, 10 (January, 1925) 214—230.

—, "Psychoanalysis and the Problem of Aesthetic Value", *International Journal of Psycho-analysis*, XXXII, 2 (1951), 73—82.

—, *Reason and Romanticism: Essays in Literary Criticism* (London, Faber & Gwyer, 1926); (Reissued New York, Russel & Russell, 1963).

—, Review of American Periodicals, *Criterion*, IV, 3 (June, 1926).

—, Review of *Johannes Scotus Erigena* by Henry Bett, *Criterion*, IV, 4 (October, 1926).

—, Review of *Principles of Literary Criticism* by I. A. Richards, *Criterion*, III, 2 (April, 1925), 444—449.

—, Review of *Science and the Modern World* by Alfred North Whitehead, *Criterion*, IV, 3 (June, 1926), 581—586.

—, Review of *Travel Diary of a Philosopher* by Count Hermann Keyserling, *Criterion*, IV, 1 (January, 1926), 189—193.

—, *The Sense of Glory: Essays in Criticism* (London, Cambridge University Press, 1929).

—, *Surrealism*, Edited with an introduction by Herbert Read, Contributions by André Breton, Hugh Sykes Davies, Paul Éluard, Georges Hugnet (London, Faber & Faber, 1936).

—, *The Tenth Muse: Essays in Criticism* (London, Routledge & Kegan Paul, 1958).

—, *The True Voice of Feeling: Studies in English Romantic Poetry* (London, Faber & Faber, 1953).

—, *Wordsworth* (London, Jonathan Cape, 1930); (Revised ed. London, Faber & Faber, 1949).

—, and Dahlberg, Edward, *Truth is More Sacred: A Critical Exchange on Modern Literature* (London, Routledge & Kegan Paul, 1961).

Some Imagist Poets: An Anthology (Boston and New York, Houghton Mifflin Co., 1915).

Some Imagist Poets: An Annual Anthology (Boston and New York, Houghton Mifflin Co., 1916).

Stead, C. K., *The New Poetic: Yeats to Eliot* (London, Hutchinson & Co., 1964).

Whitehead, Alfred North, *Adventures of Ideas* (New York, MacMillan Co., 1933).

—, *Modes of Thought* (New York, MacMillan Co., 1938).

—, *Science and the Modern World* (New York, MacMillan Co., 1926).

Worringer, Wilhelm, *Abstraction and Empathy: A Contribution to the Psychology of Style*, Translated by Michael Bullock (London, Routledge & Kegan Paul, 1953).

—, *Form in Gothic*, Authorized translation edited with an introduction by Herbert Read (London, G. P. Putnam's Sons, 1927).

INDEX OF NAMES

INDEX OF TERMS

DE PROPRIETATIBUS LITTERARUM

edited by

C. H. VAN SCHOONEVELD

Series Practica

MOUTON · PUBLISHERS · THE HAQUE

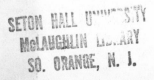